TABLE OF CONTENTS

LIST OF WITNESSES

HOUSE OF COMMONS

SESSION 1991–92

ENVIRONMENT
COMMITTEE

Second Report

COASTAL ZONE PROTECTION AND PLANNING

Volume I

Report, together with the Proceedings of the Committee
relating to the Report

Ordered by The House of Commons *to be printed*
12 *March* 1992

LONDON : HMSO
£11·85 net

The Environment Committee is appointed under SO No. 130 to examine the expenditure, administration and policy of the Department of the Environment and associated public bodies.

The Committee consists of 11 Members. It has a quorum of three. Unless the House otherwise order, all Members nominated to the Committee continue to be members of it for the remainder of the Parliament.

The Committee has power:

(a) to send for persons, papers and records, to sit notwithstanding any adjournment of the House, to adjourn from place to place, and to report from time to time;

(b) to appoint specialist advisers either to supply information which is not readily available or to elucidate matters of complexity within the Committee's order of reference;

(c) to communicate to any other such committee its evidence and any other documents relating to matters of common interest; and

(d) to meet concurrently with any other such committee for the purposes of deliberating, taking evidence, or considering draft reports.

The membership of the Committee since its appointment on 2 December 1987 has been as follows:

Sir Hugh Rossi (Chairman)

Mr John Battle
(appointed 9.5.91)
Mr Henry Bellingham
(discharged 18.3.91)
Mr Paul Boateng
(discharged 19.12.89)
Mr John Cummings
Mr Barry Field
(appointed 12.12.91)
Mr Richard Holt
(died 20.9.91)
Mr George Howarth
(appointed 19.12.89,
discharged 16.5.90)
Mr Ralph Howell
(appointed 18.3.91)
Dr Kim Howells
(appointed 16.5.90,
discharged 9.5.91)

Mr Andrew Hunter
Mr Robert B. Jones
Mr Terry Lewis
(appointed 26.10.90)
Mr Keith Mans
(discharged 18.3.91)
Mr Tom Pendry
Mr Peter L. Pike
(discharged 26.10.90)
Mr Robin Squire
(discharged 18.3.91)
Mr Anthony Steen
(appointed 18.3.91)
Mr Hugo Summerson
(appointed 18.3.91)

The cost of printing and publishing this Report is estimated by HMSO at £8,279·82.

The cost of preparing for publication the Shorthand Minutes taken before the Environment Committee and published with this Report was £5,842·39.

LIST OF MEMORANDA INCLUDED IN THE MINUTES OF EVIDENCE

LIST OF APPENDICES TO THE MINUTES OF EVIDENCE

UNPUBLISHED MEMORANDA

Additional memoranda have been received from the following organisations and have been reported to the House, but to save printing costs they have not been printed and copies have been placed in the House of Commons Library where they may be inspected by Members. Other copies are in the Record Office, House of Lords, and are available to the public for inspection. Requests for inspection should be addressed to the Record Office, House of Lords, London SW1 (telephone 071-219 3074). Hours of inspection are from 9.30 am to 5.00 pm on Mondays to Fridays:

Arun District Council

Association of National Park Officers

British Aggregate Construction Materials Industries and Sand and Gravel Association Joint Marine Panel

British Coal

British Hang Gliding Association

British Marine Industries Federation

British Railways Board

Campaign for the Protection of Rural Wales

Christchurch Borough Council

Countryside Commission

Countryside Commission for Scotland

Countryside Council for Wales

Danish Coastal Agency for Physical Planning

Danish Coast Authority

Department of Geography and Topographic Science, University of Glasgow

Department of Maritime Studies and International Transport, University of Wales

Druridge Bay Campaign

East Sussex Coastal Group, Institution of Civil Engineers

English Nature

Heritage Coast Forum

Holderness Coast Protection Joint Committee

Institute of Estuarine and Coastal Studies

Irish Sea Study Group

Kent and Essex Sea Fisheries Committee

London Boroughs Association

Marine Conservation Society

Marine Technology Directorate Ltd

Mersey Barrage Company Ltd

Ministry of Agriculture, Fisheries and Food

National Rivers Authority

National Trust

Nature Conservancy Council for Scotland

New Forest District Council

Norfolk County Council

North Norfolk District Council

North Sea Work Group/East Anglia

Pembrokeshire Coast National Park Authority

Permanent International Association of Navigation Congresses

Royal Institution of Chartered Surveyors

Royal Society for Nature Conservation

Royal Yachting Association

Science and Engineering Research Council

Shellfish Association of Great Britain

Soil Survey and Land Research Centre
    Environmental Research Centre, University of Durham

Sports Council

Suffolk Wildlife Trust

Sussex Wildlife Trust

Swansea Bay Study Group

Tayside Regional Council

Waveney District Council

Weymouth and Portland Borough Council

SECOND REPORT

COASTAL ZONE PROTECTION AND PLANNING

The Environment Committee has agreed to the following Report:

PREFACE

1. Coastal zone protection and planning cannot be reviewed in isolation; they are inextricably linked to the administration and management of the many activities and uses of the coastal zone. In this inquiry, we have therefore chosen to take a broad and integrated view of coastal issues and of the multitude of bodies including Government Departments, local authorities and public agencies which have policies, responsibilities or interests in the coastal zone[1].

2. Government officials stressed repeatedly to us that existing arrangements for coast protection and sea defence are all working "extremely well". The vast majority of witnesses in their submissions to this inquiry, however, takes rather a different view. It was significant that our request for written evidence from the Department of the Environment resulted in a memorandum that set out, *for the first time*, a full statement of the Government's policies and activities for coastal zone protection and planning.

3. From the evidence presented to us, we firmly believe that coastal protection, planning and management in the United Kingdom suffer from centuries of unco-ordinated decisions and actions at both the national and local levels. We found that there are inadequacies in legislation, anomalies in the planning system, a lack of central guidance, and overlapping and conflicting policies and responsibilities (and in some cases a lack of action) among a host of bodies, with poor co-ordination between them. Much of this has arisen partly because of the pattern of ownership of the coastal zone and partly because the boundaries separating the administrative authorities are not drawn with regard to the presence of natural coastal processes and the possible consequences on one part of the coastline by interference in another. Administrative responsibilities should match the coastal dynamics as the reverse will never happen. We conclude that ignoring this as a principle historically has led to the present general failure to plan or protect this nation's coastal resources in any integrated or co-ordinated manner.

4. The coast is subject to all manner of valid demands and uses by maritime communities, maritime-based industries and conservation and recreation bodies. Inevitably, some difficult judgements have to be made in order to protect people, properties and livelihoods, and yet to safeguard the natural coastal environment—all within the framework of physical changes of an often unspecified magnitude.

5. We believe that there is no panacea for resolving all the problems experienced in the coastal zone; different areas will require quite different treatment. We also believe that some of the problems can be tackled within the present system, for example through the provision of Government guidelines and support. However, the evidence presented to us in this inquiry has weighed heavily in favour of the need for a more comprehensive and integrated approach to be taken: legislation needs to be consolidated and updated, coastal policy developed, planning systems reviewed, and coastal zone plans developed. Above all, coastal zone protection and planning demand an overall perspective and not the *ad hoc* and sectoral approaches that have been adopted in the past.

6. The new integrated approach to protecting and planning the coastal zone is commonly known as "Coastal Zone Management". It aims to balance demands for coastal zone resources, to promote their sustainable use and, as far as is possible, to resolve conflicts of use by integrating planning and management within coastal "cells" that are defined by natural coastal processes rather than by administrative boundaries. Britain is fortunate in that it has the building blocks for an integrated Coastal Zone Management approach—the commitment of a whole range of bodies with responsibilities and influence in the coastal zone, and the existence of coastal groups and fora which can be adapted to take on new Coastal Zone Management roles. We believe that Coastal Zone Management delivered through a cascade of national, regional and local Coastal Zone Plans is the key to sustaining the present uses, enjoyment and ecological richness of the coastal zone into the future.

---

[1] *see* paragraphs 28–32 and Figure 1.

SUMMARY OF CONCLUSIONS AND RECOMMENDATIONS

Defining the " Coastal Zone "

7. We agree that the coastline should not be seen as a physical or administrative boundary, but that the coastal zone should be treated as one integrated unit, embracing inshore waters, intertidal areas and maritime land. (paragraph 17)

We conclude that definitions of the coastal zone may vary from area to area and from issue to issue, and that a pragmatic approach must therefore be taken at the appropriate national, regional or local level. (paragraph 18)

Legislation and Policy

We consider that current legislation for activities taking place within the coastal zone is too diffuse to provide an integrated or efficient framework for coastal protection and planning. We therefore recommend that this legislation be reviewed for consolidation and updating. (paragraph 19)

We await the Department's final Planning Policy Guidance Note on coastal planning with interest, and trust that it will take account of the conclusions and recommendations of this Report. (paragraph 21)

The European Community and Coastal Policy

We recommend that the Government take every opportunity to involve United Kingdom experts in the formulation and discussion of proposed EC policies and Directives on the coastal zone, and we urge the Government to put pressure on the Commission to make progress with an EC Directive on coasts. (paragraph 27)

Responsibility for the Coastal Zone and Coastal Policy

We recommend that the Government act on a review of the many organisations with an interest in the coastal zone in order to reduce unnecessary duplication of responsibilities and to improve co-ordination. (paragraph 32)

A National Coastal Zone Unit

We accept the argument that there is a need for a central unit to adopt a national overview of coastal zone policy, and we believe that the Department of the Environment should be the lead Government Department in setting up this unit. We feel that the institutional arrangements for such a unit, however, are best decided by Government. We therefore recommend that the Department of the Environment consider options for a national coastal zone unit with a view to producing a discussion paper for wide consultation. (paragraph 35)

A National Coastal Strategy

We believe there is a need to establish a national framework for the strategic planning and protection of the United Kingdom coast, urged on by forthcoming EC legislation. We recommend that the Government considers how best to formulate a national coastal strategy that sets long-term objectives and guidelines for implementing coastal policy. (paragraph 39)

Regional Coastal Groups

We recommend that coastal defence issues be addressed on a regional coastal cell basis, and that the existing Regional Coastal Groups be reorganised and resourced accordingly. In addition, we recommend that these groups be broadened in scope and membership to enable them to take on wider Coastal Zone Management as defined in paragraphs 116 and 117. (paragraph 42)

Information and Research Co-ordination

We welcome the DOE's review of earth science data needed for decision-making in the coastal zone, and we suggest that the following issues be addressed in that review:

(a) that resources be made available to map the geology of the coastal zone, and that this information is made available to planners, engineers and coastal managers;

(b) that there is support for more research into the physical and biochemical processes acting within coastal cells and the interdependencies between those cells;

(c) that there is more research into the relationships between biochemical, ecological and physical parameters in the coastal zone;

(d) that the Government explore ways of bringing together existing and newly acquired data on the coastal zone into well structured and accessible databases and geographic information systems; and

(e) that the Government, possibly through the national coastal zone unit, develop a strategic plan for future research programmes on coastal zone processes. (paragraph 45)

Control of Development and Use Above and Below the Low Water Mark

The division between the planning control systems at sea and on land may be regarded as forming the root of many of the problems with current coastal protection and planning policies. In brief, there is a failure at present adequately to link the offshore impact of onshore development or the onshore impact of offshore development. Harmonising the planning systems of below and above the low water mark seems to us to be the basic requisite for an integrated approach to planning in the coastal zone. One way to achieve this harmonisation, as recommended by many of our witnesses, is to extend the control of planning authorities beyond the low water mark. (paragraph 49)

In our view, the present divide between the landward and seaward planning systems obstructs any attempt at integrated planning of the coastal zone. We recommend that the Government give serious consideration to this dichotomy and seek ways of harmonising the two planning regimes. A blanket extension of local planning authority jurisdiction or the extension of certain planning authority powers where needed should be options that are explored. (paragraph 51)

We recommend that the Government address the issue of harmonising landward planning control and seaward planning control as far as the 12 nautical mile limit of territorial waters. (paragraph 52)

The Role of the Crown Estate Commissioners

We believe that the role of the Crown Estate Commissioners acting as both the landlord and the quasi-planning authority of the sea bed needs to be reviewed. We are content for the Commissioners to exercise their rights as landlords, but subject to a planning authority that is concerned with wider issues that affect the environment and the community at large. We therefore recommend that the Government review the role of the Crown Estate Commissioners and transfer their quasi-planning functions at sea to a more appropriate authority. (paragraph 54)

The Government View Procedure and Marine Aggregate Extraction

We recommend that those Councils which hold Section 18 Orders be placed under a statutory duty to evaluate marine aggregate extraction applications with due regard for the environmental effects of proposed operations. Such an amendment could form part of the review for consolidation and updating coastal legislation which we have recommended above. (paragraph 57)

We recommend that when the DOE carries out its review of the Government procedure for licensing aggregate extraction it should consider submitting the reports of HR Wallingford to other experts for comment. We also recommend that the NRA is included as a statutory consultee in the Government View procedure. (paragraph 61)

We recommend that the Government View procedure be reviewed in order to include an environmental assessment of marine aggregate extraction on the flora and fauna of the sea bed and adjacent areas. (paragraph 62)

We recommend that marine aggregate extraction operations should be continually monitored for their effects on sediment patterns and the environment of the coastal zone. We also recommend that in view of the lack of comprehensive information and knowledge, the broad range of physical, chemical and biological factors of each site should be specifically investigated before extraction or dredging takes place. (paragraph 63)

We recommend that a more strategic approach be developed to the extraction of marine aggregates so that account is taken of patterns of supply and demand for the materials, the availability of reserves both now and in the future, and the use and availability of alternative sources and materials. (paragraph 64)

Port and Harbour Authorities

We recommend that environmental assessments be carried out for all port and harbour activities falling within the scope of the Environmental Assessment Regulations but which are permitted under the General Development Order where those activities significantly affect the coastal zone environment or the local community. (paragraph 67)

We recommend that the Government consider how best to place environmental duties on port and harbour authorities and also duties to consult the relevant statutory bodies over any future developments that may affect the local environment. In addition, we recommend that ports should be encouraged to liaise with local communities about their activities and should be expected in particular to work with relevant coastal groups in developing Coastal Zone Management Plans. (paragraph 68)

We commend the work of the Chichester Harbour Conservancy in accommodating so many diverse interests within the one committee. We recommend that this approach be copied in other ports and harbours. (paragraph 70)

Environmental Assessment

We recommend that the Government review the application of procedures for environmental assessment within the coastal zone in order to ensure a more equitable and comprehensive coverage of the requirements. We also recommend that the Government urge the EC to review the scope of Directive 85/337/EC with respect to the coastal zone. (paragraph 73)

Responsibility for Coast Protection and Sea Defence

Prior to the establishment of a national coastal zone unit, we have much sympathy with those witnesses who believe that coastal defence policy is no longer an appropriate MAFF responsibility. We believe that the DOE would provide a more suitable lead on coastal defence issues, operating through the NRA. We recommend that the Government seriously consider the rationale for retaining coastal defence policy within the Ministry of Agriculture as part of a wider review of responsibilities for the coastal zone. (paragraph 78)

Regional Flood Defence Committees

We recommend that there should be a review of the membership and chairmanship of the Regional Flood Defence Committees to achieve a balanced representation of interests. (paragraph 79)

Internal Drainage Boards

We believe that there should be a review of the role of the Internal Drainage Boards with regard to their conservation duties. Their transfer to the NRA should be an option for consideration. (paragraph 80)

Sea level Changes and Areas at Risk

We welcome MAFF's guidance to coastal authorities on response strategies for sea level rises, but we recommend that the Government continue to monitor the implications of short-term climatic fluctuations such as storm cycles change and issue advice as information becomes available. (paragraph 82)

New topographic databases are urgently required if areas at risk from sea level rises are to be identified. We recommend that the Government ensure that this information is produced and made available to all interested parties. In addition, we recommend that the Government support the development of geographical information systems that can integrate the data necessary for predictive assessments to be made. (paragraph 84)

We recommend that the Government build on its recent advice to authorities on sea level allowances for coastal defences and issue guidance on how to manage and resource abandon and retreat policies at the coast, including the role, design and implementation of set-back lines, and how to compensate land and property owners in the areas affected. (paragraph 88)

Controlled Retreat

We believe that the concept of controlled retreat is an attractive one, but in need of further study and monitoring over the long term. We trust that the bodies which commissioned the Posford Duvivier report will seek to act on its conclusions. (paragraph 90)

We recommend that research and development be continued into the recreation of wildlife habitats from agricultural land at the coast and that monitoring of the changes in natural habitats be continued to provide a better basis of understanding for such work. (paragraph 91)

We recommend that in order for controlled retreat of coastal defences to become a realistic policy, progress be made in formulating cost/benefit analyses that include appropriate and acceptable quantifications of the environmental effects of coastal defence options. (paragraph 92)

We recommend that the Government consider ways of resourcing the creation of new coastal habitats as an incentive for landowners to participate in a policy of controlled retreat. (paragraph 93)

Financing Coastal Defences: Hard v Soft Engineering

We agree that a general preference for soft defences is to be welcomed, but this should be tempered by a need to ensure both fitness for purpose, and more fundamentally, that the design of any defence system is based on a sound knowledge of the natural processes. (paragraph 96)

We recommend that the Government continue to review its funding arrangements for coastal defence works with a view to promoting rather than discouraging the use of soft engineered schemes, and supporting the maintenance and repair as well as the capital costs of all coastal defences. (paragraph 96)

We recommend that there should be better co-ordination between those authorities responsible for dredging, disposing of and utilising marine aggregates in order to avoid the unnecessary dumping of dredged material that could be used elsewhere. In addition, we recommend that environmental impact assessments be made of the possible effects of dumping. (paragraph 97)

Nature Conservation Designations

We are disappointed that there has been no progress with protecting marine conservation areas since our recommendation on this issue seven years ago. We recommend that when the Government reviews marine conservation legislation it explore approaches other than those of Marine Nature Reserves and Marine Consultation Areas which have so far proved to be unsatisfactory and unworkable. The wider concept of Marine Protected Areas should be one of the options considered. (paragraph 101)

We are concerned that the conservation of areas below the low water mark is hampered by the inability of landward designations to straddle the land/sea divide. This problem is ultimately linked to the wider issue of planning regimes in the coastal zone, which we dealt with in previous recommendations. We recommend that in its review of marine conservation legislation, the Government address the issue of how to link conservation of land and sea areas, how to protect sites of marine conservation importance, and consider as an option extending SSSI-type mechanisms below the low water mark. (paragraph 102)

Protective Ownership of Coastal Land

We recommend that the Government actively facilitate the acquisition of coastal land by appropriate organisations, supported by sensitive management agreements as options for protecting the natural fabric of the coastal zone. Such a policy might be developed by a national coastal zone unit. (paragraph 104)

The " Urban " Coast

We believe that the conservation of the coastal zone should be a general aim, and not confined to the finest stretches of the coastline nor to the most important sites of wildlife importance. We recommend that the Government give a strong lead on the protection of the coastal resource as a whole. (paragraph 106)

Pollution

We believe that with the establishment of the proposed Environment Agency, the whole area of marine pollution control is in need of review. We therefore repeat the recommendation of our previous Report on the Environment Agency and urge the Government to consider whether responsibility for marine pollution control, which is at present dispersed across several Departments, would be better invested in one lead body, and whether the Environment Agency could fulfil that central role. (paragraph 109)

We recommend that greater effort be made to find alternative means of disposing of colliery spoil and slurry than dumping such waste in the coastal zone, and that the deadline of 1995 be made absolute and not conditional. (paragraph 110)

Fishing

We recommend that the Government seek to achieve a balance between the exploitation of fish and shellfish in the coastal zone and marine habitat and wildlife conservation. Zoning of coastal fishing waters according to sensitivity with the assistance of the Sea Fisheries Committees, the Shellfish Association of Great Britain, MAFF, the NRA and conservation bodies would be one option. (paragraph 113)

We appreciate that the regulatory procedure for fish farms has been reviewed and improved in recent years, but we believe that there is still a case for bringing fish farming within the direct control of elected planning authorities. We recommend that the Government consider the desirability of such a policy as part of a wider review of extending planning controls below the low water mark. In addition, we recommend that the environmental effects of fisheries be monitored, particularly in inshore areas. (paragraph 114)

Coastal Zone Management

We recognise the benefits of the approach known as Coastal Zone Management, and we recommend that such an approach be adopted as the framework for all coastal zone planning and management practices in the United Kingdom. (paragraph 117)

Coastal Zone Management Plans

We recommend that there should be a hierarchy of Coastal Zone Management Plans from the national to regional and local levels. We believe these Plans should be non-statutory documents, but that their policies should be incorporated in the relevant Development Plans, and that the grant-aid policies of the organisations concerned with the coast are linked to this strategic framework. We recommend that the Government issue guidance on how CZM Plans are to be prepared, by whom, and what they should cover. (paragraph 125)

Coastal Zone Management Groups

We recommend that the Government consider how best to establish, resource and empower regional Coastal Zone Management Groups based on natural coastal "cells" as the linchpin of integrated protection and planning of the coastal zone. (paragraph 131)

INTRODUCTION

Scope of Inquiry

8. While we recognise the advantages of adopting a United Kingdom perspective for coastal zone protection and planning, we decided at the beginning of this inquiry to focus on England and its shared estuaries with Scotland and Wales. Whereas this decision was made for the sake of what we could usefully achieve in the short time available to us before being overtaken by a General Election, we trust that the conclusions and recommendations of this Report have a nation-wide relevance and that they will be considered for application throughout the United Kingdom.

9. The aim of the inquiry was to investigate existing policies and responsibilities for planning and protecting the coastal zone with a view to making recommendations to Government. We found that such a review is long overdue. We received over 80 submissions of written evidence and heard oral evidence from 15 groups of witnesses, a reflection both of the importance and the diversity of the coastal zone. In order to experience issues at first hand we wished to visit coastal sites in this country[1], and in order to gain insight into different approaches to coastal problems, we also planned to travel abroad to speak to experts in France, Denmark and the European Commission in Brussels. It was with deep regret that our plans for these visits were overtaken by events as the General Election approached.

10. In view of the complexity and the specialisms involved in this inquiry, we enlisted the guidance of three Specialist Advisers, Dr Chris Fleming, Director of Sir William Halcrow and Partners Limited, Dr Susan Gubbay, Senior Conservation Officer with the Marine Conservation Society and Mr Ceri Jones, Head of the Environmental Services Division in the Planning Department of Sefton Metropolitan Borough Council. We are very grateful to them for their expert assistance.

Structure of the Report

11. Coastal zone protection and planning constitute an enormous and complex topic of inquiry. In order to manage and digest the great quantity of information we have collected, we have decided to structure our Report into six main sections. We begin with a brief account of the coastal resource and the pressures affecting the coast. The major " issues " of the coastal zone as we have identified them, we have grouped into four: those relating to the national framework; planning in the coastal zone; coast protection and sea defence; and nature conservation. For each issue, we describe the current situation, summarise the evidence we have received, and present our conclusions and recommendations. We fully recognise the linkages and interrelationships between the headings we have chosen. We end the Report with a discussion of Coastal Zone Management, its potential contribution to resolving problems in the coastal zone and the mechanisms that might need to be established to support Coastal Zone Management.

The Coastal Resource

12. When it is appreciated that nowhere in the United Kingdom is more than 135 km (84 miles) from the sea[2], that the United Kingdom's 15,000 km[3] (about 9,500 miles) of coast is much larger in relation to land area than that of most other countries[4], and that the United Kingdom has approximately one-third of a million square km (125,000 square miles) of territorial waters[5], it is not surprising that coastal issues are of particular significance.

13. The coastal zone of the British Isles has a rich diversity of flora, fauna and landscape, a reflection of the range of its geological and geomorphological features, its climatic variability and its tidal ranges. For example, we were told by the Royal Society for the Protection of Birds (RSPB) that " the United Kingdom's estuaries are among the most biologically productive systems in the world "[6], and by the Joint Nature Conservation Committee (JNCC) that " the marine communities

---

[1] We were able to visit United Kingdom coastal sites in Sefton MBC. We had hoped to visit the Hampshire coast, Chichester Harbour and relevant organisations in those areas such as the County Council and SCOPAC, but constraints on time prevented this.

[2] Evidence p 2.

[3] About 18,600 km (11,500 miles) at high water when all the tidal inlets and larger islands are included, (Appendix 15).

[4] Evidence p 2.

[5] Susan Gubbay *A Future for the Coast?* 1990, WWF and MCS.

[6] Evidence p 108.

around Great Britain are the most diverse of any European Atlantic state's border "[1]. The extent and depth of the coastal wildlife resource have been well documented in the submissions we received from both these organisations and from English Nature[2].

14. The value of the coast stretches wider than its wildlife, however. Fish, marine aggregates, oil and gas reserves, natural harbours, a varied landscape for recreation, water for industrial cooling, tidal and wind power are all part of the coastal resource.

Pressures on the Coast

15. The coastal zone is subject to increasing pressure of all kinds. The natural resources of the coastal zone support the livelihood of many people. Many more use the coast for recreation, while the coast offers attractive locations for commercial, housing and leisure developments. By virtue of its natural resources, then, the coastal zone has to bear the competing pressures of fishing, fish farming, shell fishing, ports and harbours, navigation, sport and recreation, coastal settlements, sand dredging, marine aggregate extraction, oil and gas extraction, land claim and coastal engineering, conventional and renewable energy installations, waste disposal from land- and sea-based sources, landscape and wildlife conservation.

16. Underlying this concentration of human activity, the coastal zone is subject to the shifting dynamics of physical processes and change. The coastal environment will probably be the first to encounter the effects of possible sea level rises as a result of climate change, and it always has experienced and always will experience the impact of marine erosion and accretion, tectonic movement, storm effects and flooding. To a large extent, the ability of the coastal zone to sustain all these human and physical pressures will depend on how its natural fabric is protected, planned and managed. We turn now to the problems and issues involved in achieving effective protection, planning and management of the coastal zone.

---

[1] Appendix 15.
[2] Evidence pp 108, 152, Appendix 15.

THE NATIONAL FRAMEWORK

Defining the "Coastal Zone"

17. It would seem appropriate that we begin by defining what we mean by the "coastal zone". We were informed by the Marine Conservation Society, that while there is no universally accepted definition of the coastal zone, there is widespread support for including in it elements of coastal land, the intertidal zone[1] and the adjacent sea[2]. This holistic view was shared by several witnesses, including the Department of the Environment[3], the Joint Nature Conservation Committee[4], Sefton Metropolitan Borough Council[5], the Centre for Marine Law and Policy[6] and the local authority associations[7]. The Institution of Civil Engineers[8] defined the coastal zone as "the foreshore and the nearshore area, together with areas where leisure activities, construction or industry could affect the regime of the shoreline". The Countryside Commission quoted from the European Workshop on Coastal Zone Management[9] which stated that the coastal zone is

> "a dynamic human and natural system which extends to seawards and landwards of the coastline. Its limits are determined by the geographical extent of the natural processes and human activities which take place there"[10].

We agree that the coastline should not be seen as a physical or administrative boundary, but that the coastal zone should be treated as one integrated unit[11], embracing inshore waters, intertidal ares and maritime land.

18. We realise that for planning and management purposes, the coastal zone may have to be defined more precisely, an issue to which we return in paragraph 119. While it is tempting to spend a great deal of time discussing the length and breadth of the coastal zone both inland and out to sea, we share the view of the Marine Conservation Society that precise definitions should not be seen as a priority task[12]. Rather, if the focus is on the coastal problem or issue of concern, the geographic extent of the affected zone will largely define itself. Obviously, an element of judgement will be involved to decide how much of a land or sea area is appropriate to dealing with as many coastal issues as possible, while being aware of influences outside the boundaries. As a result, **we conclude that definitions of the coastal zone may vary from area to area and from issue to issue[13], and that a pragmatic approach must therefore be taken at the appropriate national, regional or local level[14].**

Legislation and Policy

19. There are over 80 Acts dealing with the regulation of activities taking place in the coastal zone[15]. Even issues as closely linked as coast protection and sea defence[16] are split between four Acts—the Coast Protection Act 1949, the Land Drainage Act 1976, the Food and Environment Protection Act 1985 and the Water Act 1989. We received evidence from Wildlife Link which criticised the "loopholes and anomalies in the law concerned with the coastal zone"[17]. The Institution of Civil Engineers, on the other hand, told us that "there is probably enough legislation

---

[1] Intertidal land is the land between the high and low water marks.

[2] Evidence p 82.

[3] Evidence p 2.

[4] Appendix 15.

[5] Evidence p 253.

[6] Appendix 8.

[7] Appendix 4.

[8] Evidence p 222.

[9] The Workshop was held at Poole, United Kingdom from 21–27 April 1991.

[10] Evidence p 168.

[11] Evidence pp 40, 82, 132, Appendix 4.

[12] Susan Gubbay, 1991, *A Definition of the "Coastal Zone" for United Kingdom Coastal Management Programmes*, Discussion Paper CZM/1, Marine Conservation Society, WWF.

[13] Evidence p 2.

[14] This conclusion has also been reached by the Australian Parliament's House of Representatives Standing Committee on Environment, Recreation and the Arts, April 1991, *The Injured Coastline: Protection of the Coastal Environment*, Australian Government Publishing Service, Canberra, paragraph 1.9.

[15] Appendix 8.

[16] The DOE defines coast protection as the protection of land from erosion or encroachment by the sea, and sea defence as the prevention of flooding of land by rivers or the sea, Evidence p 14.

[17] Evidence p 125.

but it actually needs consolidation "[1]. When we asked MAFF as to progress on updating or consolidating the Coast Protection and Land Drainage Acts[2], we were told that the legislation relating to water had been consolidated and the other two had been amended to take account of various changes as a result of the establishment of the NRA[3]. We believe that the importance of this legislation requires similar treatment to the Water Acts or Planning Acts in terms of consolidation and updating. In any case, the Acts will be in need of amendment as a result of changes in relation to the establishment of the proposed Environment Agency[4]. **We consider that current legislation for activities taking place within the coastal zone is too diffuse to provide an integrated or efficient framework for coastal protection and planning. We therefore recommend that this legislation be reviewed for consolidation and updating.**

20. As regards policy for the United Kingdom's coastal zone, there appears to be no national framework. The Government's White Paper on the Environment " This Common Inheritance "[5] was criticised by both the Royal Institution of Chartered Surveyors[6] and by the Royal Town Planning Institute as giving "scanty attention. . .to a vital environmental resource, the coastline "[7]. The Government's First Year Report[8] also contained little on coastal policy. In view of this perceived deficiency in Britain's Environmental Strategy we are encouraged that the Department of the Environment has recently published a Policy Planning Guidance Note[9] which mentions the coast and coast protection issues as subjects to be taken into account in statutory land use Development Plans. This Planning Policy Guidance also refers to the need for consideration to be given to the sustainability of development. In its submission to us, the Government stated that it was necessary to balance environmental and development interests on the coast on a " sustainable basis "[10]. A working definition was provided for us by Dr Derek Langslow of English Nature[11], who referred to the Ramsar Convention which defines " sustainable use " in terms of " a use which meets the needs of the present generation while maintaining its potential to meet the needs and aspirations of the future generations ". He suggested that " one is looking to ensure that there are no irreversible changes which damage that long-term future, and that there is an attitude and a commitment towards those natural systems which allows that ". This thread runs through many of the discussions we have had with witnesses in this inquiry, and it is significant that it is being specifically recognised in current land use planning policy. We return to the question of sustainable use in our discussion of Coastal Zone Management[12].

21. We welcome the fact that the concept of sustainable development has been incorporated (although not named as such) in the draft Planning Policy Guidance (PPG) on coastal planning which the DOE published on 11 March 1992[13]. We also welcome the PPG's support for " conferences of local planning authorities on a regional or, where appropriate, an inter-regional basis "[14]. We have had no time to consider the document in detail, but we are disappointed that the PPG makes no mention of how these regional conferences should ideally be organised on a natural coastal cell basis; neither does it address the issue of harmonising planning policy above and below the low water mark. We note that on the important question of coastal conservation, the draft PPG refers to the newly published Planning Policy Guidance on nature conservation[15], but this companion PPG fails to address adequately the issue of marine conservation and how the United Kingdom is to implement its international obligations below low water mark. **We await the Department's final Planning Policy Guidance Note on coastal planning with interest, and trust that it will take account of the conclusions and recommendations of this Report.**

---

[1] Q 682.

[2] Consolidation was recommended by the Welsh Affairs Committee in its Report on the Towyn Floods (HC 426 1989–90) and considered " desirable " by the Government in its response (Cm 1451).

[3] Q 164.

[4] HC 55 1991–92.

[5] Cm 1200, September 1990, HMSO, London.

[6] The Royal Institution of Chartered Surveyors (Evidence not printed).

[7] Evidence p 33.

[8] Cm 1655, September 1991, HMSO, London.

[9] DOE, February 1992, PPG 12, *Development Plans and Regional Planning Guidance.*

[10] Evidence p 2.

[11] Q 402.

[12] *See* Paragraph 117 below.

[13] Paragraphs 1.2, 1.13, 2.10, 2.19.

[14] Paragraph 3.2.

[15] Planning Policy Guidance on Nature Conservation, draft dated 18 February 1992.

The European Community and Coastal Policy

22. The problems facing the coastal zone have received international attention. In the same way that pollution respects no international or administrative boundaries, the coastal zone demands cross-frontier agreements where coastlines and estuaries are shared. The European Community has become more involved in coastal issues, beyond that of pollution of coastal waters. The Council of Europe adopted a resolution on the protection of coastal areas in 1973. In 1981, the Conference of Peripheral Marine Regions adopted a European Coastal Charter, while action programmes have been initiated for countries on both the Mediterranean and the Atlantic Seaboards[1]. The Commission has had a presence at recent conferences on coastal conservation[2] and Ministerial Conferences on the North Sea[3].

23. While EC policy and legislation for the coast have developed in piecemeal fashion (for example, nature conservation Directives do not deal specifically with coastal sites), this approach is rapidly changing. We were informed by a letter from Mr Olivier Bommelaer of Directorate General XI of the European Commission in Brussels that the Commission is preparing a "comprehensive strategy on integrated management and planning of the Community coastal zones"[4], which is currently in its final stages of internal discussions. The Dutch presidency proposed a Council Resolution on these same lines, and this was adopted on 13.12.91[5]. We were informed that this matter is likely to be given "special support" by the Portuguese presidency in the first half of 1992[6].

24. From an article written by Laurens Jan Brinkhorst, Director General for the Environment[7], we can see that the Commission is strongly in favour of a "global strategy for the coastline" to achieve "ecologically sustainable development of the coastline and its resources"[8]. More significantly, the article proposes a "legal instrument" defining coastal areas and making it compulsory to draw up strategic plans for each coastal area along the whole Community coastline.

25. The Director General's thinking appears to be very much in line with ours when he expresses concern over pressures affecting the coast; the lack of legal instruments in most Member States and the EC to devise and implement a coastal strategy; no existing global tool for integrated management of the coastal environment; and sectoral provisions in national legislation scattered across several laws and upheld by many different bodies with unco-ordinated objectives.

26. Although at an evolutionary stage, the Director General's ideas confirm many of the conclusions we had already reached in our inquiry. For example, he supports the notion of sustainable use of the coastal zone; treating the coastal zone as one unit, and not as two distinct land and sea environments; integrated coastal zone management at national, regional and local levels; and the co-ordination of data, knowledge and research programmes.

27. If EC policy is to be drafted along the lines the Director General has indicated, we believe it is imperative that British expertise plays a major role in that process. The importance of the United Kingdom taking a lead in Europe in the development of coastal strategies and planning policies was emphasised by the RTPI in its evidence to us[9]. We believe that United Kingdom initiatives, on which we have received submissions from many authorities and agencies, have much to offer our European partners, and we would hope that the United Kingdom's forthcoming Presidency of the European Council[10] will help the United Kingdom to develop its profile in this area. **We recommend that the Government take every opportunity to involve United Kingdom experts in the formulation and discussion of proposed EC policies and Directives on the coastal zone, and we urge the Government to put pressure on the Commission to make progress with an EC Directive on coasts.**

---

[1] COM(89)598 Final and COM(91)354 Final.

[2] European Workshop on Coastal Management, Poole, April 1991, and European Coastal Conservation Conference in the Hague, November 1991.

[3] Third International Conference on the Protection of the North Sea in the Hague on 7 and 8 March 1990.

[4] Appendix 10.

[5] Council of Ministers, Press Release 229, 12.12.91 p 17.

[6] Appendix 10.

[7] L. J. Brinkhorst, "Prospects for a Community Strategy" in *Natureuropa* 11/91.

[8] *ibid.*

[9] Evidence p 35.

[10] The United Kingdom's Presidency will commence on 1.7.92 for a period of six months.

Responsibility for the Coastal Zone and Coastal Policies

28. It is partly because the land and sea areas of the coast have been planned and managed separately, partly because there has been no central direction on coastal policy, and partly because the range of issues within the coastal zone is so wide and has traditionally been compartmentalised that there has developed a multitude of organisations with a responsibility or interest in the coast. The range of central Government Departments, Agencies and statutory bodies concerned with coastal policies and various major uses of the marine environment is illustrated in Figure 1[1].

FIGURE 1

Central Government Departments, Agencies and Statutory Bodies concerned with various major uses of the marine environment

Alkali & Radiochemical Inspectorate (N.I)	HM Customs & Excise
Council for Nature Conservation & the Countryside	HM Industrial Pollution Inspectorate (Scotland)
Countryside Commission	HM Inspectorate of Pollution (England/Wales)
Countryside Commission for Scotland	Home Office
Countryside Council for Wales	Ministry of Agriculture Fisheries & Food
Crown Estate	Ministry of Defence
Department of Agriculture (N.Ireland)	National Rivers Authority
Department of Economic Development (N.Ireland)	Nature Conservancy Council for Scotland
Department of Energy	Natural Environment Research Council
Department of the Environment	Northern Ireland Office
Department of the Environment (N.Ireland)	River Purification Boards
Department of Trade & Industry	Science & Engineering Research Council
Department of Transport	Scottish Office, Agriculture & Fisheries Dept
English Nature	Scottish Office, Environment Department
Foreign & Commonwealth Office	Sports Council
Health & Safety Executive	Welsh Office

SPECIFIC AREAS OF INTEREST	
NATURE & LANDSCAPE CONSERVATION	Council for Nature Conservation & Countryside Countryside Commission Countryside Commission for Scotland Countryside Council for Wales Department of the Environment Department of the Environment (N.Ireland) English Nature Nature Conservancy Council for Scotland Natural Environment Research Council Scottish Office Environment Dept Welsh Office
FISHERIES/HARVESTING/AQUACULTURE	Crown Estate Department of Agriculture (N.Ireland) Department of Transport Foreign & Commonwealth Office Health & Safety Executive Ministry of Agriculture Fisheries & Food Scottish Office, Agriculture & Fisheries Dept
MILITARY USE	Ministry of Defence

---

[1] Appendix 1 (updated) of Susan Gubbay, 1990, *Op cit.*

MINERAL/ENERGY EXTRACTION	Crown Estate Department of Agriculture (N.Ireland) Department of Economic Development (in N.Ireland) Department of Energy Department of Trade and Industry Department of Transport Foreign and Commonwealth Office Health and Safety Executive Ministry of Agriculture Fisheries & Food Scottish Office, Environment Dept Scottish Office, Agriculture & Fisheries Dept
WASTE DISPOSAL/POLLUTION CONTROL	Alkali and Radiochemical Inspectorate (in N.Ireland) Department of Agriculture & Fisheries for Scotland Department of Agriculture (N.Ireland) Department of Energy Department of the Environment Department of the Environment (N.Ireland) Department of Trade & Industry Department of Transport Health & Safety Executive HM Industrial Pollution Inspectorate (in Scotland) HM Inspectorate of Pollution (in England & Wales) Home Office Ministry of Agriculture Fisheries & Food National Rivers Authority (England & Wales) Natural Environment Research Council River Purification Boards (Scotland) Scottish Office, Environment Dept Welsh Office
RECREATION	Council for Nature Conservation & the Countryside Countryside Commission Countryside Commission for Scotland Countryside Council for Wales Department of Education & Science Department of the Environment (N.Ireland) Department of Transport Home Office Scottish Office, Environment Dept Sports Council Welsh Office
ENGINEERING WORKS	Department of Agriculture and Fisheries for Scotland Department of Energy Department of Transport Ministry of Agriculture Fisheries & Food National Rivers Authority Science & Engineering Research Council
SHIPPING/NAVIGATION/COMMUNICATIONS	Crown Estate Department of Energy Department of the Environment (N.Ireland) Department of Trade & Industry Department of Transport Foreign and Commonwealth Office HM Customs & Excise Ministry of Defence Science & Engineering Research Council

29. At the second and third "tiers" of responsibility, local authorities have a prominent role in the landward part of the coastal zone; they have powers under the Planning Acts, extensive statutory environmental regulation functions and the ability to make bylaws. They also have rights to be consulted by bodies such as the National Rivers Authority, Her Majesty's Inspectorate of Pollution, English Nature, the Countryside Commission and their Welsh and Scottish equivalents[1].

30. More specifically, the local authority associations provided us with details of their coastal responsibilities[2]. County Councils have responsibility for strategic planning, minerals and waste planning, environmental education, waste disposal, highway planning and construction. District Councils' responsibilities include development control, local plan preparation, coast protection, and the provision of services (litter clearance, refuse collection, operation of tourist facilities, parks

[1] Evidence p 2.
[2] Appendix 4.

maintenance) on amenity beaches and elsewhere. Metropolitan Authorities are responsible for the majority of these county and district functions. Finally, all three types of authority have other responsibilities which affect the coastal zone, such as management of land in their ownership, environmental improvement work, pollution control, emergency planning and countryside services.

31. In addition to the bodies mentioned, there are many other organisations with coastal interests or responsibilities. They include private sector landowners, Harbour and Port Authorities, Sea Fisheries Committees, the National Trust, English Heritage, the Rural Development Commission, the Tourist Boards and several National Park Authorities.

32. In all, it has been estimated that as many as 240 Government Departments, local authorities and public agencies at national and local level have some sort of responsibility for the United Kingdom's coastal zone[1]. To these may be added hundreds of parish councils in England and Wales. As a result, "control and responsibility in the coastal zone is therefore often seen as being fragmented and confused"[2]. Other ingredients to the "recipe for confusion"[3] include varying jurisdictions for different bodies for specific issues, as Figure 2 shows[4]; a perceived lack of communication and consultation between those bodies which can lead to conflict and poor co-ordination[5]; as well as confusion and a lack of understanding as to their specific roles and powers[6]. We received many submissions calling for some review of the complex division of responsibilities with a view to rationalising the number of agencies involved and to streamlining processes for policy formulation and implementation[7]. Indeed, Mr McQuail from the Department of the Environment told us that he was "sure it would be possible to reduce the number" of cooks, and that this issue was "actively under consideration"[8]. **We recommend that the Government act on a review of the many organisations with an interest in the coastal zone in order to reduce unnecessary duplication of responsibilities and to improve co-ordination.**

A National Coastal Zone Unit

33. Much of the problem of a lack of co-ordination and duplication between agencies with coastal responsibilities could be resolved if there were a stronger Government lead. Figure 1 has shown that there is no one Government Department that currently takes the lead for coastal policies. We received much criticism of the current system whereby "the civil servants seem to be able to cobble together arrangements between them"[9]. That there is no clear central responsibility for coasts was evident also from the Government witnesses that appeared before the Committee: Mr McQuail, Deputy Secretary for Planning, Rural Affairs and Built Heritage in the DOE introduced himself as responsible "among other matters, for countryside and wildlife issues, for planning issues and one or two other things not directly relevant"[10].

34. We received a considerable body of evidence that recommended the establishment of a single body to provide a central lead[11]. As illustration, we were told by the WWF[12]

"The whole situation is extremely complex and frequently confusing. A national strategy for the coastal zone headed by one lead agency would help to resolve much of the current confusion and resultant lack of management".

The RTPI, on the other hand, while "opposed to the creation of a super body"[13], believed that the Department of the Environment should assume overall responsibility for decisions at a national level[14]. Organisations such as the Marine Conservation Society argued the need for a Coastal Zone Management Unit[15] which would provide a focus for developing integrated management of the

---

[1] Evidence p 90.

[2] Evidence p 226.

[3] Evidence p 90.

[4] Taken from Susan Gubbay, 1990, *Op cit*.

[5] Evidence pp 35, 111.

[6] Evidence p 225, Appendix 3.

[7] Evidence pp 90, 125, 171, Appendices 4, 7, 19, Association of National Park Officers (Evidence not printed).

[8] Q 7.

[9] Q 270.

[10] Q 1.

[11] Evidence pp 85, 90, 117, 226, Appendices 2, 3, 8, Institute of Estuarine and Coastal Studies, Royal Institution of Chartered Surveyors (Evidence not printed).

[12] Evidence p 139.

[13] Evidence p 40.

[14] Q 77.

[15] Evidence p 85.

FIGURE 2

Jurisdiction of various organisations in the coastal zone on specific issues

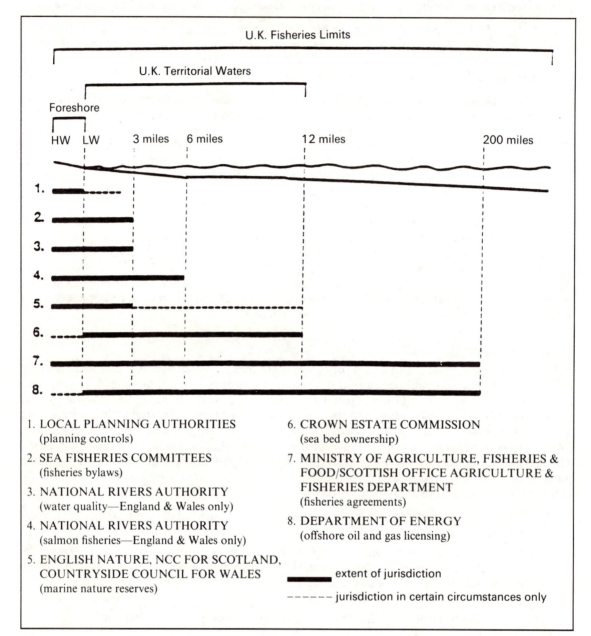

1. LOCAL PLANNING AUTHORITIES
   (planning controls)

2. SEA FISHERIES COMMITTEES
   (fisheries bylaws)

3. NATIONAL RIVERS AUTHORITY
   (water quality—England & Wales only)

4. NATIONAL RIVERS AUTHORITY
   (salmon fisheries—England & Wales only)

5. ENGLISH NATURE, NCC FOR SCOTLAND,
   COUNTRYSIDE COUNCIL FOR WALES
   (marine nature reserves)

6. CROWN ESTATE COMMISSION
   (sea bed ownership)

7. MINISTRY OF AGRICULTURE, FISHERIES &
   FOOD/SCOTTISH OFFICE AGRICULTURE &
   FISHERIES DEPARTMENT
   (fisheries agreements)

8. DEPARTMENT OF ENERGY
   (offshore oil and gas licensing)

━━━━━━ extent of jurisdiction

------ jurisdiction in certain circumstances only

coastal zone, draw together the many agencies with coastal reponsibilities, and act as a link into European and international coastal matters. The Society provided us with a discussion paper they had prepared with the WWF[1] which put forward three options for a Coastal Zone Management Unit: a new free-standing agency; a separate agency operating under the auspices of the DOE; or a Unit within the DOE. The RSPB favoured

> " a discrete well resourced Unit to be established within central Government to take the lead on coastal matters. Such a Unit should be charged with co-ordination of marine and coastal management and planning at a national strategic level. It should be able to integrate the activities of the various sectors of Government and develop comprehensive consultation and implementation mechanisms for the sustainable use of the coastal zone "[2].

Other witnesses such as the National Trust, Countryside Commission and Institution of Civil Engineers[3] supported the concept of some kind of national co-ordinating unit, but had no strong views as to where it should be located. When we asked witnesses whether the National Rivers Authority could fulfil the role of a national coastal zone unit, the response was a tepid one. As we were told by the RSPB[4], the NRA's responsibilities include only some aspects of the coastal zone (coastal erosion, flood defence, water quality). The NRA's role is an issue to which we return in paragraph 78. When we asked the DOE about a national coastal zone unit, the officials appeared strongly opposed to the creation of any new central body, believing that a single agency " would not in itself solve the problem "[5].

35. We agree with the majority of witnesses that there needs to be clearer responsibility and better co-ordination for coastal issues at a national level, and that the coastal expertise in several Government Departments needs to be brought together. We are reluctant, however, to support the creation of yet another bureaucratic tier of responsibility for the coastal zone. In that respect, we found that the proponents of a national coastal zone unit shared our objection[6]. As we were told by the Marine Conservation Society, another tier does not have to be created if the unit is " an integrating function within what happens at present, with a much more identifiable basis "[7], or as the National Trust said, it did " not think we see any unit as having any great function on the ground. Many of the functions will continue to be fulfilled by the local authorities "[8]. **In conclusion, we accept the argument that there is a need for a central unit to adopt a national overview of coastal zone policy, and we believe that the Department of the Environment should be the lead Government Department in setting up this unit. We feel that the institutional arrangements for such a unit, however, are best decided by Government. We therefore recommend that the Department of the Environment consider options for a national coastal zone unit with a view to producing a discussion paper for wide consultation.**

36. The possible functions of a national coastal zone unit need to be part of this consultation exercise, but we perceive they should include developing a national strategy for coasts, co-ordinating research and information, and providing a framework and supporting the work of regional coastal zone groups. The unit might also be identified as the authority requiring environmental assessments for certain uses within the coastal zone. These are all issues which we discuss in more detail below.

37. We know that a more integrated approach to coastal policy and responsibility is pursued in Denmark in the form of its Kyst Inspektoral (Danish Coast Authority), and we received from the British Embassy in Copenhagen, literature about coastal zone protection and planning in that country[9]. The Danish Coast Authority is concerned with coast protection; coastal planning is the

---

[1] Marine Conservation Society *A Coastal Zone Management " Unit " for the United Kingdom*, Discussion Paper, MCS and WWF.

[2] Evidence p 106.

[3] QQ 268, 433, 766.

[4] Q 353.

[5] Q 6.

[6] QQ 269, 270.

[7] Q 270.

[8] Q 269.

[9] Per Roed Jakobsen and Niels Tougaard, 1991, *Coastal Zone Planning and Erosion Management in Denmark*, Danish Coast Authority, Lemvig, and *The Danish Coasts: status of and information on current coastal strategy work*, Ministry of the Environment National Agency for Physical Planning, Copenhagen.

responsibility of the National Agency for Physical Planning. We found it remarkable that the DOE was only just " making inquiries " about other countries' arrangements for coastal policy, and that the findings of that survey are still overdue [1].

A National Coastal Strategy

38. While in the United Kingdom, Planning Policy Guidance for coasts is most welcome and overdue, we realise that by definition, a PPG Note is at present limited to *land*, and is not sufficient to fill the role of a strategy which provides a common base of aims or priorities at a national level. We know that the EC is already attempting to synthesise its laws and policies for coastal areas with a Directive that will mean compulsory coastal strategies for Member States. The United Kingdom needs to prepare for this. Even the DOE owned to adopting an *ad hoc* approach to coastal policy, although Mr McQuail preferred to call the approach an " incremental " one[2]. We received evidence from many witnesses that criticised the lack of a national coastal strategy[3]. Many also called for Government guidance to achieve consistency of approach to coastal policies[4]. We appreciate the DOE's view that because of its diversity, the coastline needs to be addressed by " a range of policies dealing case by case, aspect by aspect and problem by problem with the issues "[5]. However, we do not see that an attention to local detail obviates the need for a national framework. Rather, the amount of evidence presented to us contradicts the DOE's comment that " the case has not been made and . . . it is unsustainable for a single national policy or strategy "[6]. As we were told by the Countryside Commission[7], their work would be " greatly helped by a national strategy for the coast ".

39. It is often the case that perceptions vary over what is or is not a " strategy ". We would not favour some weighty document that sets out detailed policies for the whole of the British coastline. But we do believe that there is a need for a strategic statement to indicate the Government's policies and priorities for coasts, to guide the allocation of national resources, and to aid the development of regional and local coastal strategies. **In conclusion, we believe there is a need to establish a national framework for the strategic planning and protection of the United Kingdom coast, urged on by forthcoming EC legislation. We recommend that the Government considers how best to formulate a national coastal strategy that sets long-term objectives and guidelines for implementing coastal policy.**

Regional Coastal Groups

40. In the context of a national strategy and a national coastal zone unit, we have been persuaded by many witnesses that coastal zone protection and planning need to be co-ordinated at a regional level[8]. We were informed by the Institution of Civil Engineers (ICE) that although provision was made in the Coast Protection Act 1949 for the Government to form collaborative groups and joint committees, these provisions have never been used[9]. In the last five years, however, there have developed voluntary Regional Coastal Groups concerned with coastal engineering, which pool information and address coastal problems of mutual interest. There is also a number of other regional groups such as the Dorset Marine Forum and Cardigan Bay Forum which have a broader-based membership. There are currently some 18 Regional Groups where the emphasis is on coastal engineering in England and Wales, with another two in Scotland[10], in all covering about 98 per cent of the coast[11] as Figure 3 shows[12]. We received evidence from several of the Regional Coastal Groups[13]. We were told that last year MAFF recognised the benefit of liaising with these Groups and held a meeting with representatives[14]. In addition, meetings are hosted at the ICE headquarters once or twice a year in order to exchange information and ideas.

[1] Q 23.

[2] Q 20.

[3] Evidence pp 35, 85, 90, 113, 132, 135, 158, 171, 226, Association of National Park Officers (Evidence not printed).

[4] Evidence pp 40, 85, 113, 158, 171, 225, 253, Appendices 4, 8, 12.

[5] Q 5.

[6] *ibid.*

[7] Q 442.

[8] Evidence pp 41, 85, 157, 228, Appendices 7, 11, 15, Swansea Bay Study Group (Evidence not printed).

[9] Evidence p 225.

[10] Q 710.

[11] Q 234.

[12] Based on a map provided by Waveney District Council.

[13] Anglian Coastal Authorities Group, East Sussex Coastal Group, Holderness Coast Protection Joint Committee, Standing Conference on Problems Associated with the Coastline, Swansea Bay Study Group.

[14] The list of members is included in Appendix 22 Annex A.

FIGURE 3

**Regional Groups concerned with
Coastal Engineering (as of January 1992)**

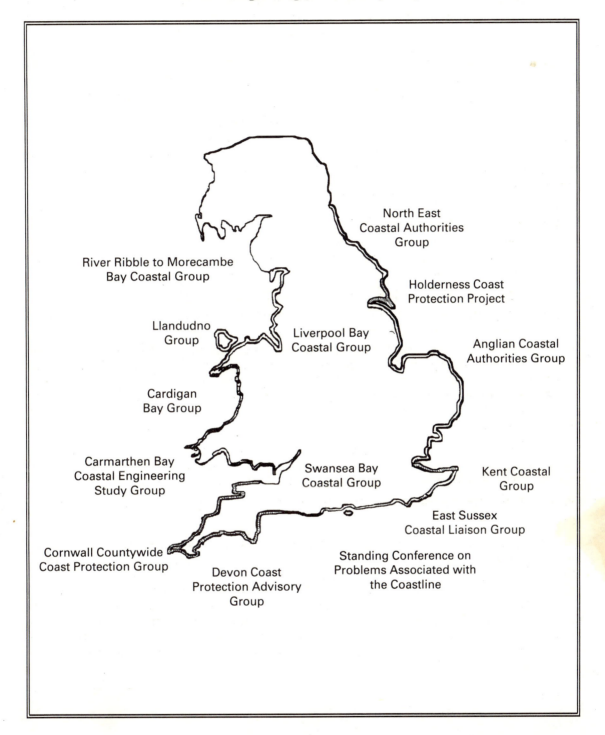

41. We commend the initiative of coastal authority engineers in establishing Regional Coastal Groups, and we appreciate the important role they play in collectively funding information and research on the coastal zone in their areas. We are aware that coastal schemes ill-constructed in the past can have a detrimental impact on the shoreline elsewhere and that coast erosion problems can simply be shifted along the coast as a result of poor co-ordination between different authorities[1]. We are aware also of the problems caused by different coastal authorities pursuing conflicting coastal policies on shared coastlines or in estuaries[2].

---

[1] East Sussex Coastal Group (Evidence not printed).
[2] Q 383.

42. We are concerned, however, that the focus of the Regional Groups is on coastal defence and engineering issues[1], commonly referred to as "Shoreline Management". While "Shoreline Management" provides a useful framework for the strategic planning of hazard protection in the coastal zone, it does not always consider interrelationships with other issues. As we state in our opening paragraph, coastal defence cannot be viewed in isolation. In addition, we heard that most of the Groups are currently based not so much on the natural coastal "cell" structure, as on administrative boundaries, which may be tidier but are less effective in addressing problems of a hydraulic or sedimentological nature[2]. English Nature informed us that a recent study commissioned by MAFF has defined seven to 10 coastal sedimentary cells that are relatively but not completely independent of one another around the English and Welsh coasts, and that a further report will produce a more definitive statement in the near future[3]. We return to the subject of regional coastal zone management groups in paragraphs 126 to 131. **We recommend that coastal defence issues be addressed on a regional coastal cell basis, and that the existing Regional Coastal Groups be reorganised and resourced accordingly. In addition, we recommend that these groups be broadened in scope and membership to enable them to take on wider Coastal Zone Management as defined in paragraphs 116 and 117.**

Information and Research Co-ordination

43. There appear to be two main problems with existing information and research arrangements for coastal zones—there are significant gaps, and what there is is unco-ordinated[4]. As the local authority associations told us

> "the marine environment is not particularly well researched, while information which has been collected is neither collated or referenced in one place, nor necessarily shared or co-ordinated between agencies"[5].

This criticism is particularly true for the shallow water environment, where the amount spent on research is totally out of proportion with that spent on deep sea processes. Other witnesses drew attention to the need for a European coastal database[6], while still others called for more ecological inventories of the coastline[7]. In particular there appears to be an absence of geological data of much of the sea bed between the low water mark and the -10 m contour[8]. As we were told by the British Geological Survey

> "the coastal zone is in geoscience terms perhaps the most poorly understood and imperfectly documented part of Britain . . . [which] results in an inadequate knowledge base to support effective Coastal Zone protection and planning"[9],

and by NERC, "the necessary data for safe and environmentally sound development remains sparse for many areas"[10].

44. We received evidence also of the lack of general knowledge about the cumulative impact of coastal activities such as offshore mineral extraction and fishing[11], while other evidence pointed to gaps in knowledge about sediment processes as they occur generally and within and between regional "cells"[12]. The ICE presented to us a long list of issues in need of research and long-term monitoring, and its own views on how that information could be collected and co-ordinated[13]. In summary, lack of information and unco-ordinated information are criticisms that may be applied across the spectrum of the coastal sciences, whether physical, chemical, biological, social, ecological or geological, and they are crticisms that apply at all levels, whether national, regional or local.

---

[1] Appendix 11.

[2] Q 702.

[3] Q 383.

[4] Evidence pp 228, 254, Appendices 1, 2, 15, 16.

[5] Appendix 4.

[6] Appendix 15.

[7] Heritage Coast Forum, Pembrokeshire Coast National Park Authority (Evidence not printed).

[8] Appendices 4, 16, East Sussex Coastal Group (Evidence not printed).

[9] Appendix 6.

[10] Appendix 16.

[11] Appendix 4, Permanent International Association of Navigation Congresses (Evidence not printed).

[12] Christchurch Borough Council, Holderness Coast Protection Joint Committee, Swansea Bay Study Group (Evidence not printed).

[13] Q 727.

45. We were disappointed to hear that there has been no progress on establishing a national co-ordinating committee to develop a coastal research strategy, as recommended by the Inter-Agency Committee for Marine Science and Technology[1]. We understand that other countries such as the Netherlands have a far better system for collecting data from various sources and making them available to users[2]. In the light of the United Kingdom's patchy and opportunistic approach to coastal information and research, we were encouraged to learn that the Natural Environment Research Council is establishing its Land Ocean Interaction Study (LOIS)[3] and that the DOE has recently commissioned a two-year research project that will identify the earth science information that is needed for making sound planning and management decisions in the coastal zone. **We welcome the DOE's review of earth science data needed for decision-making in the coastal zone, and we suggest that the following issues be addressed in that review:**

(a) **that resources be made available to map the geology of the coastal zone, and that this information is made available to planners, engineers and coastal managers;**

(b) **that there is support for more research into the physical and biochemical processes acting within coastal cells and the interdependencies between those cells;**

(c) **that there is more research into the relationships between biochemical, ecological and physical parameters in the coastal zone;**

(d) **that the Government explore ways of bringing together existing and newly acquired data on the coastal zone into well structured and accessible databases and geographic information systems; and**

(e) **that the Government, possibly through the national coastal zone unit, develop a strategic plan for future research programmes on coastal zone processes.**

[1] Q 725.
[2] Q 738.
[3] Q 741, Appendix 16.

PLANNING IN THE COASTAL ZONE

Control of Development and Use Above and Below the Low Water Mark

46. In paragraph 17 we discussed the interactions between land and sea at the coast and the widespread support for treating the coastal zone as one integrated unit. The irony is that planning and management of the land and water environments have evolved in isolation of each other. There is one planning system above the low water mark and another regime for the adjacent inshore waters.

47. The different systems operating above and below the low water mark are explained in detail in Gubbay, 1990[1] and in the evidence submitted by the DOE[2]. Briefly, the town and country planning system regulates activities and uses on the landward side of the coastal zone and is implemented (in England and Wales) by county councils at a strategic level, and at a local level by district councils. The jurisdiction of these local planning authorities generally ends at low water. The exceptions include South Wight District Council which can control offshore dredging adjacent to its coast, and the Shetland and Orkney Island Councils which have certain planning powers out to the limit of territorial waters[3]. Many port and harbour authorities also fall outside the remit of local government planning.

48. For the seaward side of the coastal zone, about half of the foreshore and most of the sea bed out to the 12-mile limit is vested in the Crown[4]. There are exceptions for certain areas of tidal land, examples of which were listed for us by the Crown Estate Commissioners[5]. As landlords they license certain activities and lease areas of foreshore and sea bed. The most relevant of these activities to this current inquiry are marine aggregate extraction, which takes place mainly in England and Wales and marine fish farming, affecting mainly Scotland.

49. **The division between the planning control system at sea and on land may be regarded as forming the root of many of the problems with current coastal protection and planning policies. In brief, there is a failure at present adequately to link the offshore impact of onshore development or the onshore impact of offshore development. Harmonising the planning systems of below and above the low water mark seems to us to be the basic requisite for an integrated approach to planning in the coastal zone. One way to achieve this harmonisation, as recommended by many of our witnesses, is to extend the control of planning authorities beyond the low water mark[6].**

50. There are 30 local councils which hold Section 18 Orders under the Coast Protection Act 1949 which allow them to control the extraction of sea bed sediments within three miles of their coastline, although South Wight is the only one which, to our knowledge, actively uses those powers[7]. We were also informed by the RSPB that planning power extension of a different kind has already been tried and tested in the Northern Isles of Scotland. In the Society's opinion, the procedures for development control in the coastal zone in Shetland and Orkney " set a helpful precedent for the rest of the United Kingdom ", and the " success of the system . . . demonstrates that there should be no real obstacles to extending the planning role of local authorities to cover the whole coastal zone "[8].

51. When we sounded the DOE on the possibility of extending planning control, officials responded that it " does not seem a practical solution "[9]. In its written evidence, the Department had defended existing arrangements on the grounds that

> " there is a much smaller variety of development below the low water mark, and less direct conflict between uses competing for available space. Furthermore, there are aspects of activity below the low water mark which have no analogy on land, for instance the historic right of free navigation "[10].

[1] Susan Gubbay, 1990, *Op cit.*

[2] Evidence pp 4–9.

[3] Susan Gubbay, 1990, *Op cit.*

[4] Evidence p 6.

[5] Evidence p 182.

[6] Evidence pp 62, 85, 91, 111, 254, Appendices 4, 7, 8, 11, 12, 15, 17, 19, Countryside Commission for Scotland, Countryside Council for Wales, London Boroughs Association, Pembrokeshire Coast National Park Authority, Weymouth and Portland BC (Evidence not printed).

[7] Q 516.

[8] Evidence p 112.

[9] Q 35.

[10] Evidence p 6.

The Crown Estate Commissioners were not opposed to extending planning control out to sea for certain activities, but had reservations[1]; offshore marine aggregate extraction they felt was irrelevant to coastal communities and beyond the resources of the planning authorities to handle. We fail to see what is impractical about treating the sea bed as "submerged land", an opinion shared by the Royal Town Planning Institute[2]. And if planning authorities can deal with issues like public rights of way, aggregate extraction and multiple use on land, they should be able to cope with rights of navigation and extraction at sea. Like the Crown Estate Commissioners[3], however, we appreciate that local authorities would need to acquire sufficient expertise to carry out the new duties that extending their jurisdiction out to sea would place upon them. **In our view, the present divide between the landward and seaward planning systems obstructs any attempt at integrated planning of the coastal zone. We recommend that the Government give serious consideration to this dichotomy and seek ways of harmonising the two planning regimes. A blanket extension of local planning authority jurisdiction or the extension of certain planning authority powers where needed should be options that are explored.**

52. Extending planning authority jurisdiction out to sea begs a further question as to how far? Three main administrative boundaries have been suggested to us—three nautical miles (the seaward extent of "controlled waters" and United Kingdom territorial waters until 1987), six nautical miles (the seaward extent of those fishing rights exclusive to the United Kingdom), and 12 nautical miles (the current limit of United Kingdom territorial waters). There are no clear cut environmental factors to distinguish between each of these limits[4], distance is "in some way a movable feast", as we were told by Sefton MBC[5], because it will depend on the problem being dealt with beyond low water mark[6]. However, it will be necessary that any planning system fully covers estuary mouths and includes off-shore islands[7], and we see the benefits of setting a comprehensive zone of coverage rather than creating a sub-zone of three miles within United Kingdom territorial waters[8]. **We recommend that the Government address the issue of harmonising landward planning control and seaward planning control as far as the 12 nautical mile limit of territorial waters.**

The Role of the Crown Estate Commissioners

53. The role and specific responsibilities of the Crown Estate Commissioners in managing the Crown Estate are explained in the memoranda we received from the Government and from the Commissioners themselves[9]. These responsibilities stem from the Crown Estate Act of 1961, under which the Commissioners have the general duty " to maintain and enhance the value of the estate, and the return obtained from it. . . .subject to the responsibility to have due regard to the requirements of good management "[10].

54. The present role of the Crown Estate Commissioners generated a considerable amount of concern among many of our witnesses[11]. We heard criticisms relating to its lack of public accountability, its poor environmental record, its dual role as both poacher and gamekeeper or judge and jury of offshore activity, its emphasis on financial gain, and its exemption from any requirement to consult organisations like the NRA. The Commissioners are obviously sensitive to the criticism they attract. It was significant that their written evidence to us stated that they

" have no particular wish to act in any quasi-planning role, provided that an appropriate planning authority can be established "[12].

When we questioned the Commissioners as to what would constitute an " appropriate " planning authority, we were told that their preference was for marine planning to be handled on a functional

---

[1] Q 505.

[2] Q 127.

[3] Q 485.

[4] Susan Gubbay, 1991, *Op cit.*

[5] Q 805.

[6] *ibid.*

[7] Q 304.

[8] Q 307.

[9] Evidence pp 6, 179–180.

[10] Evidence p 179.

[11] Evidence pp 41, 83, 91, 116, 137, 172, 227, Appendices 4, 8, 12, Pembrokeshire Coast National Park Authority, Royal Institution of Chartered Surveyors (Evidence not printed).

[12] Evidence p 179.

basis[1]. We were surprised with this answer because many other witnesses have criticised the sectoral decision- and policy-making approach as one of the major problems with current arrangements in the marine environment[2]. **We believe that the role of the Crown Estate Commissioners acting as both the landlord and the quasi-planning authority of the sea bed needs to be reviewed. We are content for the Commissioners to exercise their rights as landlords, but subject to a planning authority that is concerned with wider issues that affect the environment and the community at large. We therefore recommend that the Government review the role of the Crown Estate Commissioners and transfer their quasi-planning functions at sea to a more appropriate authority.**

55. If, as we have recommended, a planning system were to be adopted at sea, it would not be unprecedented for the Crown Estate to become bound by it. When we questioned the Commissioners as to their activities on land, we discovered that although they do not require planning permission for their development proposals, they voluntarily follow the procedures in Part IV of DOE Circular 18/84[3]. These procedures mirror those of an ordinary planning application except that instead of granting or refusing permission, the local planning authority indicates whether or not it objects to the proposal. Unresolved objections are referred to the Secretary of State for the Environment, if necessary following a public inquiry. We were informed by the Crown Estate Commissioners that there have been no cases where they have developed on land without a valid planning permission[4].

The Government View Procedure and Marine Aggregate Extraction

56. The non-statutory Government View procedure is used to control the extraction of marine aggregates. When applications for production licences are made to the Crown Estate Commissioners, they informally consult interested parties and the applications are advertised in the local papers and the fishing trade press. The consultation responses are passed to the DOE (or Welsh or Scottish Offices) which then formulates the Government View by in turn consulting other Government Departments whose interests are affected by the proposals. The Crown Estate does not issue a licence if there is a negative Government View, and accepts in every case any conditions included in a favourable View by incorporating them in the licence[5].

57. We were informed that as a non-statutory system, the Government View procedure has to give way to the system operated by South Wight District Council which we described in paragraph 50[6]. While we understand that the Council is operating a cautious licensing system for dredging in its jurisdiction, this may not necessarily have been the case in the past or indeed in other local authorities. **We recommend that those Councils which hold Section 18 Orders be placed under a statutory duty to evaluate marine aggregate extraction applications with due regard for the environmental effects of proposed operations. Such an amendment could form part of the review for consolidation and updating coastal legislation which we have recommended above.**

58. Although the Government View procedure was revised in 1989 following extensive consultations with all interested parties, we heard that there are still reservations about the new system. The Commissioners themselves admitted that "the existing system is capable of improvement"[7], and would prefer

> "a simplified system which could be statutorily based, perhaps similarly to onshore planning procedures and, perhaps, with a public inquiry process; and with the ultimate decision being seen to be taken by the Secretary of State for the Environment"[8].

The British Aggregate Construction Materials Industries (BACMI) and the Sand and Gravel Association (SAGA) criticised the Government View procedure for lacking a strict timetable, for allowing any Government Department to veto an application, and for being unclear as to whether

---

[1] Q 485.

[2] Evidence pp 89, 132, 253, Appendices 4, 8, Association of National Park Officers, Swansea Bay Study Group (Evidence not printed).

[3] (WO 37/84), Q 496.

[4] Q 498.

[5] Evidence p 6.

[6] Q 518.

[7] Q 485.

[8] Q 485.

environmental assessments should accompany applications or not[1]. They concluded that "the current Government View procedure has failed but. . .it is too soon to scrap it", and have recommended amendments accordingly.[2]

59. In contrast, we were told by English Nature that the Crown Estate Commissioners "operate a very correct and cautious approach"[3], although it is difficult to draw any meaningful trend from the figures on licence applications that we were given by the Commissioners for the last 10 years[4] (see Figure 4).

60. The Government View procedure includes the arrangement whereby the Crown Estate seeks the technical advice of a private company known as HR Wallingford[5] on any possible coastal erosion effects of an application to extract aggregate[6]. It became apparent to us during our evidence sessions with officials from MAFF, the Crown Estate, BACMI and others that the Government View procedure, the licensing decisions of the Crown Estate, and the exploration and exploitation decision of the marine aggregate industry rely solely on the work of HR Wallingford; the conclusions reached by HR are never scrutinised for second opinion. We fully accept that HR Wallingford's work is of a very high standard. Nevertheless, this reliance on a single agency concerns us because assessing the effects of marine aggregate extraction is not an exact science. When we suggested that alternative views could be sought, the response from MAFF officials was a favourable one[7]. In similar fashion, when we suggested that the NRA also should have the opportunity of commenting on aggregate extraction applications, we were met by another favourable response[8]. The sole reliance of the aggregate licensing system on HR Wallingford caused our Chairman to visit that company to observe the work carried out there[9].

61. We have no doubt that the staff of HR Wallingford are experts in their field, and we were impressed at the amount of work and research undertaken by the company. There is an obvious concentration of engineering expertise, but we understand that the company is beginning to diversify into other areas of research[10]. We remain of the opinion, however, that the Government View procedure should not rely solely on assessments prepared by one company. **We recommend that when the DOE carries out its review of the Government procedure for licensing aggregate extraction it should consider submitting the reports of HR Wallingford to other experts for comment. We also recommend that the NRA is included as a statutory consultee in the Government View procedure.**

62. During our scrutiny of the Government View procedure we also established that its main focus is the effect on patterns of marine sediment and to a lesser extent on marine life of commercial interest; the broader ecological effects of marine aggregate extraction are never considered, and there is certainly no public inquiry procedure in which conservation interests are allowed to be represented. We found that there is much concern among environmentalists about the impact of marine aggregate extraction on marine wildlife, a situation that is not helped by the apparent confusion surrounding the need for environmental assessments to accompany applications[11]. BACMI and SAGA witnesses told us that they would welcome clearer guidance from the Government on this issue[12]. **We recommend that the Government View procedure be reviewed in order to include an environmental assessment of marine aggregate extraction on the flora and fauna of the sea bed and adjacent areas.** We understand, however, that HR Wallingford does not at present use its expertise to assess the likely effects of an operation on aspects such as fishing grounds[13]. We would welcome any development which would encourage HR Wallingford to use its expertise to carry out environmental assessments as we have indicated.

[1] Evidence p 201.
[2] Evidence pp 201–202.
[3] Q 411.
[4] Q 510.
[5] HR Wallingford was formed in 1982 to take over and extend the work of the DOE's Hydraulics Research Station.
[6] Q 243.
[7] Q 252.
[8] Q 255.
[9] Appendix 29.
[10] *ibid.*
[11] Evidence p 202.
[12] Q 565.
[13] Appendix 29.

FIGURE 4

Government View summary over last 10 years

YEAR	NO. OF NEW PRODUCTION APPLICATIONS TO CROWN ESTATE	NO. REJECTED BEFORE GOVERNMENT VIEW	FAVOURABLE GV RECEIVED	UNFAVOURABLE GV RECEIVED	NO. OF GV OUTSTANDING (cumulative)	NO. OF LICENCES ISSUED
					3 at 31.12.1981	
1982	5	1	1	NIL	6	1
1983	7	1	5	NIL	7	2
1984	1	NIL	2	NIL	6	2
1985	3	NIL	3	NIL	6	5
1986	3	1	3	NIL	5	1
1987	1	NIL	2	NIL	4	2
1988	5	NIL	2	1	6	8
1989	6	1	1	NIL	10	6
1990	8	2	2	NIL	14	-
1991	6	NIL	1	NIL	19	8
TOTAL	45	6	22	1	19*	35

* 18 are still at Informal Government View Stage, 1 at the Welsh Office

Information as at 14 February 1992

63. In fact, we were concerned to find that the whole area of the impact of marine aggregate extraction on the coastal zone is under-researched, and based on premises years out of date. For example, we heard that " the action of the sea on the sea bed in depths greater than 18 metres has little or no effect "[1], a premise that has been used to justify extraction in such areas based on experiments carried out nearly 20 years ago at one site. HR Wallingford admitted that 18m is no more than a useful benchmark, and that each site should instead be assessed on its merits[2]. We heard from BACMI and SAGA representatives that there is little general research on the sedimentological effects of extraction[3]. We heard also that the findings of site-specific research carried out by HR Wallingford off the Worthing coast were being applied to the case of Great Yarmouth[4]. When we questioned the ICE about the validity of applying research results in this way, we were told that the extrapolation of study findings from one area to another could be misleading if the same conditions were not experienced[5]. **We recommend that marine aggregate extraction operations should be continually monitored for their effects on sediment patterns and the environment of the coastal zone. We also recommend that in view of the lack of comprehensive information and knowledge, the broad range of physical, chemical and biological factors of each site should be specifically investigated before extraction or dredging takes place.**

64. Finally, we wish to comment on the general attitude of the marine aggregate industry to its responsibilities towards the marine environment. BACMI and SAGA witnesses stressed repeatedly that the environmental impact of their operations was no worse than those of the fishing or port and harbour industries[6]. We comment more fully on the fishing industry in paragraphs 111 to 114, but we see no merit in industries justifying their own environmental record against the default of others. In addition, given that marine aggregates are a finite resource, we were disconcerted to hear that it is only since 1986 that the Crown Estate and the DOE have carried out regional assessments of the aggregate reserves around the coast[7], that such assessments are insufficient[8], and that little research into developing alternative sources of construction material appears to be undertaken[9]. We believe that the aggregate industry needs to adopt a more responsible approach to its environmental impact, a subject upon which BACMI and SAGA representatives themselves confessed they needed guidance[10]. **We recommend that a more strategic approach is developed to the extraction of marine aggregates so that account is taken of patterns of supply and demand for the materials, the availability of reserves both now and in the future, and the use and availability of alternative sources and materials.**

Port and Harbour Authorities

65. There are about 300 harbours around the coast of Great Britain, each an important generator of employment and contributor to the local and national economies. The complex planning arrangements under which ports and harbours operate are described in the DOE's memorandum of evidence[11] and in a supplementary note we received from the Department of Transport[12]. Briefly, most harbour authorities require planning permission for their development proposals, but they benefit from permitted development rights under the Town and Country Planning General Development Order 1988[13]. As we have noted previously[14], however, development in ports and harbours below the low water mark falls outwith the jurisdiction of the town and country planning system. There are yet further exemptions such as harbour authorities which are also Crown bodies, and in these cases procedures are the same as those described in paragraph 55.

---

[1] Q 544.

[2] Appendix 29.

[3] Q 546.

[4] Q 533.

[5] Q 758.

[6] QQ 559, 561, 658.

[7] Q 528.

[8] Q 754.

[9] Q 584.

[10] Q 625.

[11] Evidence p 8.

[12] Appendix 23.

[13] Permitted development rights include developments relating to operational land of harbours, dredging in harbours, and lighthouses and other navigational aids, Q 645.

[14] *See* Paragraph 47 above.

66. Several witnesses have criticised port and harbour authorities' permitted development rights and other exemptions[1]. The RTPI, for example, expressed some concern that ports and harbours

> "ought then to be subject to the normal rigours of planning control. They should not have *carte blanche* to do all things within harbour and port areas"[2].

The National Trust also saw "no reason" why ports and harbours should enjoy exemptions. Rather,

> "they should be subject to the same environmental impact assessment criteria as any other development. Indeed perhaps more so, because many of these developments are large and therefore they could conceivably have a larger impact"[3].

67. A related issue to permitted development rights is that developments under the GDO are also exempt from Environmental Impact Assessment (EIA) Regulations[4]. Sefton planning officers alerted us to the kind of problems that can arise with permitted development rights when they showed us the example of loose coal being stored in the Port of Liverpool, immediately adjacent to a housing area. We were told that as a result of sustained local pressure, the Mersey Docks and Harbour Company has given the undertaking to Parliament to carry out environmental assessments on such projects, but the planners believed that local solutions like this are "not a very satisfactory" approach to a widespread problem[5]. **We recommend that environmental assessments are carried out for all port and harbour activities falling within the scope of the Environmental Assessment Regulations but which are permitted under the General Development Order where those activities significantly affect the coastal zone environment or the local community.**

68. We take the point made in the evidence submitted by the British Ports Federation[6] that much of the problem with port-related activity stems from residential development adjacent to port areas and consequent complaints regarding air and noise pollution from those who have come recently to a previously existing nuisance. We share the Federation's concern that new developments should not take place in areas where an obvious incompatibility exists with existing land use and industrial activity. However, we also understand that the substantial exemption from planning powers of port-related activities presents local Councils with considerable difficulties in trying to maintain environmental standards in areas surrounding ports, and that local communities have no redress against the activities of ports. We were encouraged to hear from the British Ports Federation that progress is being made to establish regular dialogue between ports, local authorities and local residents[7]. **We recommend that the Government consider how best to place environmental duties on port and harbour authorities and also duties to consult the relevant statutory bodies over any future developments that may affect the local environment. In addition, we recommend that ports should be encouraged to liaise with local communities about their activities and should be expected in particular to work with relevant coastal groups in developing Coastal Zone Management Plans.**

69. The other main concern we have relating to ports and harbours is the potential environmental effect of recent legislation to privatise port authorities[8]. We were informed of the Felixstowe Docks case[9] in which the docks were expanded, destroying part of the conservation value of the Orwell Estuary Site of Special Scientific Interest (SSSI). As a result of loss of trade, the expanded dock facilities were not required. When we questioned the British Ports Federation whether an overview of port development might be beneficial, we were told that decisions to develop a port are best taken locally by the port concerned[10]. We see the merit of this, but future port developments should be tested by public inquiry within the planning system.

70. Finally, we are aware that ports and harbours can be planned and managed in harmony with other activities and uses of the coastal zone. Chichester Harbour was recommended to us as a model for all other port areas, not least because it has a harbour conservancy with very strong environmental duties, statutory powers relating to moorings, zonings and wildlife sanctuaries,

---

[1] Evidence pp 115, 252, Appendices 4, 12.
[2] Q 145.
[3] Q 326.
[4] Appendix 28 contains details of Environmental Assessment arrangements for harbours.
[5] Q 811.
[6] Evidence p 214, Q 652.
[7] QQ 646, 652.
[8] Ports Act 1991.
[9] Evidence p 128.
[10] Q 680.

effective consultations and linkages with local authorities, and an effective committee structure on which local interests are well represented[1]. **We commend the work of the Chichester Harbour Conservancy in accommodating so many diverse interests within the one committee. We recommend that this approach be copied in other ports and harbours.**

Environmental Assessment

71. Much stress was laid by a number of witnesses[2] on the value of and reliance on the formal procedures for the assessment of the environmental impact of various developments which were established by the EC Directive 85/337/EEC. This Directive is implemented in the United Kingdom by a series of Regulations[3] covering Harbour Works[4], Fish Farming[5], Flood Defence[6] and Town and Country Planning[7]. Developments carried out under Parliamentary Bill procedures or the new Ministerial Order procedures[8] are also subject to formal environmental assessment (EA). Nevertheless, in the course of our inquiry we came across several gaps and inconsistencies in the coverage and application of these Regulations.

72. There is some doubt as to whether coast protection works *per se* are covered by the Regulations at all[9]. This seems to be an omission in the Directive itself and so a matter for Government to take up directly with the EC. The potentially damaging effects of certain fishing operations are also not covered by the Directive. There is confusion about who should require an assessment to be carried out on marine aggregate extraction proposals[10]. The Crown Estate Commissioners have been identified as the " competent authority " for this purpose in respect of fish farming proposals[11]. This in itself is not an entirely satisfactory situation in view of the Crown Estate's status as landlord. Although port authorities must submit an EA for harbour development proposals, they are exempt from such requirements for any " port-related " development within the port area by virtue of permitted development rights under the General Development Order 1988. It has also been pointed out that port dredging proposals are exempt from EA[12]. On land, Circular 15/88 sets out " indicative criteria " which show when EA may be needed, but the coast is not recognised as a particularly sensitive area where otherwise conventional developments may well warrant EA[13].

73. These examples indicate a rather patchy approach to the evaluation of the environmental impact of a range of developments in the coastal zone. This situation would seem to vitiate the Government's professed intention to " balance economic and other interests with environmental and safety factors on a sustainable basis "[14]. **We recommend that the Government review the application of procedures for environmental assessment within the coastal zone in order to ensure a more equitable and comprehensive coverage of the requirements. We also recommend that the Government urge the EC to review the scope of Directive 85/337/EEC with respect to the coastal zone.**

---

[1] Q 367.

[2] Evidence pp 4, 6, 150, 172, 181.

[3] DOE/WO, 1989, *Environmental Assessment: a Guide to the Procedures,* HMSO.

[4] Harbour Works (Assessment of Environmental Effects) Regulations 1988, SI No 1336 and Harbour Works (Assessment of Environmental Effects) (No 2) 1989, SI No 424.

[5] Environmental Assessment (Salmon Fishing in Marine Waters) Regulations 1988, SI No 1218.

[6] Land Drainage Improvement Works (Assessment of Environmental Effects) 1988, SI No 1217.

[7] Town and Country Planning (Assessment of Environmental Effects) Regulations 1988, SI No 1199.

[8] Evidence p 9.

[9] QQ 146, 167–177, Appendices 25, Annex B, 27.

[10] Q 506.

[11] Evidence p 6.

[12] Appendix 26.

[13] Evidence p 253, Q 826.

[14] Evidence p 2.

COAST PROTECTION AND SEA DEFENCE

Responsibility for Coast Protection and Sea Defence

74. Responsibility for coastal defence policy (which embraces both coast protection and sea defence) lies with MAFF[1]. Under the Coast Protection Act 1949, maritime district councils carry out coastal protection works that have been approved by the appropriate Minister. Councils must consult the NRA, neighbouring maritime district councils, the county council, harbour, conservancy and navigation authorities and fisheries committees and MAFF (for licensing under the Food and Environment Protection Act 1985) before submitting proposals to MAFF. This applies to all works except maintenance, repair and emergency works. MAFF then consults other Government Departments, the Crown Estate, and in England, the Countryside Commission and English Nature. The full consultation process is described in the DOE's submission[2].

75. As regards flood defence, the Land Drainage Act 1976 and the Water Act 1989 provide for the construction, improvement and maintenance of defences against inland and coastal flooding in England and Wales to be undertaken by the NRA through its 10 Regional Flood Defence Committees, by local authorities, and by some 250 Internal Drainage Boards[3]. The NRA informed us that a recent survey of sea defences (which comprise some 1,214 km of the coastline in England and Wales) has been carried out, details of which appear in its evidence[4]. It is apparent from this survey that extensive lengths of the coastline are owned by private individuals and by organisations like British Rail and the Ministry of Defence.

76. We are aware that the National Audit Office is currently carrying out an investigation into sea defence and coast protection in England, in particular whether there are soundly based programmes for coastal defence; whether those schemes are properly selected, evaluated and prioritised, including their impact on the environment; and whether coastal defences are adequate and individual schemes implemented successfully with regard to time, cost, quality and impact. We trust that our conclusions and recommendations will complement the findings of the NAO and the eventual scrutiny of the Public Accounts Committee.

77. Although existing arrangements appear clear on paper and, in MAFF's view, " the present system in general works extremely well "[5], we have received several submissions that have criticised the responsibilities in practice.[6] The substance of these criticisms is that it is often difficult to distinguish between coast protection and sea defence, that the arrangements can be complex when they are split between MAFF, NRA and the local authorities, and how inappropriate it is that coastal defence should be vested in an agricultural Government Ministry when the majority of defences protect urban land and interests. Many sea defences do directly protect agricultural land, but are justified on the basis that a breach in those defences could lead to flooding of higher value urban areas or infrastructure inland. We were therefore urged to consider whether coastal defence should be brought under one Act of Parliament and under a single body.

78. We have some sympathy for considering coast protection and sea defence works as a single issue in that both seek, through engineering techniques, to defend coastal land from the action of the sea. We have already recommended that the Government should formulate proposals for a national coastal zone unit[7]. Such a unit would, in the long-term, assume responsibility for policies affecting the coastal zone, and as a result, coastal defence might be one of its functions. **Prior to the establishment of a national coastal zone unit, we have much sympathy with those witnesses who believe that coastal defence policy is no longer an appropriate MAFF responsibility. We believe that the DOE would provide a more suitable lead on coastal defence issues, operating through the NRA. We recommend that the Government seriously consider the rationale for retaining coastal defence policy within the Ministry of Agriculture as part of a wider review of responsibilities for the coastal zone.**

---

[1] Or in Wales, with the Welsh Office.

[2] Evidence p 14.

[3] *ibid.*

[4] Evidence p 59.

[5] Q 162.

[6] Evidence pp 41, 93, 118, 173, 251, Appendices 2, 3, 4, 12, 14, 19, Christchurch BC, Institute of Estuarine and Coastal Studies (Evidence not printed).

[7] *See* Paragraph 35 above.

Regional Flood Defence Committees

79. We received evidence from the RSPB that called into question the role and function of the NRA's Regional Flood Defence Committees (RFDCs)[1]. The RFDCs are executive committees of the NRA in that they have the final authority to determine which sea defence and land drainage schemes proceed. We consider it essential that such committees exist to represent local interests in the planning and location of defence works. However, where we do take issue is with the constitution of the RFDCs. We cannot accept that the " token " environmental representation on these committees is sufficient to balance the well-established farming interests which have given exemplary service over many years[2]. **We conclude that there might well be advantages in reviewing the membership and chairmanship of the Regional Flood Defence Committees to achieve a balanced representation of the various interests.**

Internal Drainage Boards

80. Internal Drainage Boards provide and operate drainage works, pumps and sluices behind the sea walls in some low lying coastal areas. They have come under criticism from the RSPB for, in some cases, damaging or destroying important nature conservation sites[3]. We heard from MAFF that Internal Drainage Boards (IDBs) " work very well indeed "[4], and that much effort has been made to produce conservation guidelines for those bodies. We inquired whether the functions of the IDBs could be transferred to the NRA. MAFF " supposed " the functions could[5]; the NRA thought itself " the logical organisation " to take over the IDBs' responsibilities if such a policy were agreed, although there would be resource implications which would have to be assessed[6]. **We believe that there should be a review of the role of the Internal Drainage Boards with regard to their conservation duties. Their transfer to the NRA should be an option for consideration.**

Sea level Changes and Areas at Risk

81. At the beginning of this inquiry, local authority witnesses were expressing some concern that they were confused over how to meet the as yet undefined challenges of possible sea level rise or climatic change. They said they would welcome Government advice on how to prepare for the future[7]. As other witnesses pointed out, however, it is not only sea level rises that pose problems; how to protect the coast from extreme storm conditions[8], and the potential intrusion of marine-derived groundwater into coastal aquifers used for freshwater extraction[9] are also issues for concern. We appreciate that local and other authorities such as the NRA need to programme their capital financing over decades, and that annual public spending rounds will not be adequate to handle long-term issues such as climatic change[10]. We therefore asked MAFF what Government guidance is being prepared. We were referred to the report of the Intergovernmental Panel on Climate Change (IPCC)[11], which makes predictions for " global " sea level rise.

82. The predictions of the IPCC are explained in a supplementary memorandum we received from the DOE[12]. IPCC was not able to make predictions for regional sea level rise " because of the state of development of computer modelling "[13]. However, based on a combination of the " IPCC Best Estimate trend " for global sea rise and predictions for earth crustal movement in Great Britain (such as tilting[14]), MAFF has produced guidance to authorities for the design of coastal defences. This guidance, dated November 1991, is included in the supplementary evidence submitted at our request by the DOE[15]. The allowances for the design of coastal defences are based

---

[1] Evidence p 118.

[2] Q 213.

[3] Evidence p 118.

[4] Q 216.

[5] Q 218.

[6] Q 225.

[7] Evidence p 253, Appendices 3, 4.

[8] Appendix 8.

[9] Appendix 16.

[10] Appendix 17.

[11] *Scientific Assessment of Change*, Report of Working Group I to the Intergovernmental Panel on Climate Change, WMO and UNEP, July 1990. The IPCC was established by the United Nations Environmental Programme and the World Meteorological Organisation.

[12] Appendix 22 Annex C.

[13] Q 57.

[14] Appendix 16.

[15] Appendix 22 Annex G.

on NRA regions and are reproduced in Figure 5. We note that these figures are based on sea level rises up to 2030, and that some change in predictions may occur for defences that have an effective life beyond that year. **We welcome MAFF's guidance to coastal authorities on response strategies for sea level rises, but we recommend that the Government continue to monitor the implications of short-term climatic fluctuations such as storm cycles and issue advice as information becomes available.**

FIGURE 5

Allowances for sea level rise

NRA Region	Allowance
Anglian, Thames, Southern	6 mm/year
North West, Northumbria	4 mm/year
Remainder	5 mm/year

83. Now that authorities have been advised of regional sea level rises, there is a need to identify which coastal areas are at risk and to develop policies for them[1]. This would involve a complex process of zoning coastal lowland into risk categories based on topography and the appropriate sea level rise allowance[2], and the development of geographical information systems that can integrate tidal, flood defence, sea level, land use and census data, a process that has already been started by the NRA. As we were informed by the Environmental Research Centre at the University of Durham[3], it is not easy to define flood risk areas on low lying land because in some areas Ordnance Survey altitudinal data is some 20 years old, and because the + 5 m contour is the lowest shown on 1:25,000 maps, except in the Fenlands and Teeside where the zero contour is plotted.

84. It is not just the coastal authorities who need to be able accurately to identify areas at risk presently or potentially from coastal flooding or erosion. We received evidence from the Flood Hazard Research Centre at Middlesex Polytechnic that pointed to the inadequacies of the property market. Legal searches do not always pick up the risks of flooding, erosion or ground instability, and sellers have been known to be economical with the truth—market failures which then create strong local pressure for the affected properties to be protected[4]. Similarly, we heard from the Association of British Insurers that the risk of increased flood and storm damage as a result of climatic change is a serious concern in future insurance policies. The Association told us that " the absence of an authoritative analysis of the relative vulnerability to flooding of different coastal areas, linked to postcodes, prevents the use of predictive assessments "[5], and as a result, the ABI was considering the commissioning of its own research on these issues. **New topographic databases are urgently required if areas at risk from sea level rises are to be identified. We recommend that the Government ensure that this information is produced and made available to all interested parties. In addition, we recommend that the Government support the development of geographical information systems that can integrate the data necessary for predictive assessments to be made.**

85. Sea level rise has serious implications for planning policy in the areas affected. We were told by the Flood Hazard Research Centre, for instance that the options for responding to sea level rise are " protect, retreat or abandon "[6]. Adaptation is another[7]. Abandonment and retreat both require management to avoid planning and investment blight. For example, investment could be made in areas to be abandoned without the knowledge of any planned abandonment; on the other hand, knowledge of future abandonment may result in premature abandonment through

---

[1] Evidence p 228, Appendices 3, 12, 17.

[2] Environmental Research Centre, University of Durham (Evidence not printed).

[3] *ibid.*

[4] Appendix 11.

[5] Appendix 2.

[6] Appendix 11.

[7] Adaptation would include building storm shelter, modifying local building regulations.

withdrawal of investment; or people may be trapped in property for which they can find no purchaser. The Flood Hazard Research Centre also drew attention to the location of nuclear power stations on coastal sites for which response policies will also need to be drawn up, an issue which we know has attracted recent press interest[1].

86. There appears to be some controversy over planning policies for areas at risk. We were told by some witnesses that local planning authorities should be able to refuse planning permission in threatened areas without the DOE overruling on appeal, and should be given powers to award compensation in those cases[2]. The NRA was keen to ensure that any development in a flood plain does not increase the risk of flooding[3]. The East Sussex Coastal Group recommended that any development permitted which enjoys the protection of coastal defence should contribute towards the future cost of maintaining that scheme[4]. The University of East Anglia and Norfolk and Suffolk Broads Authority recommended that planning permission should be refused in areas of erosion, but could be granted in flood hazard zones conditional upon specified building measures[5].

87. We were interested to hear that Norfolk County Council's submitted Structure Plan is one of the first in the United Kingdom to propose policies that are justified on the inevitability of coastal erosion and sea inundation[6]. In the Council's opinion, protection of the eroding coast (currently about one metre a year in the north-east of the County) is not only " too costly to be realistic ", but is also " environmentally unacceptable and would cause damage to beaches elsewhere by depriving them of material "[7]. In consequence, the Structure Plan submitted to the Secretary of State for the Environment includes policies for a presumption against new building in areas likely to be affected by marine erosion within the expected lifetime of the development; a presumption against development on land to the seaward side of sea defences (including holiday chalets and caravans); and a presumption against development in areas liable to flooding unless the standard of defence is appropriate to the development proposed[8].

88. The first of Norfolk's policies introduces the concept of " development setback policy ", which may be new to the United Kingdom, but is, we understand, integral to coastal planning strategies in other parts of the world. In the United States of America for example, 11 coastal states now have formal setback policies[9]. Denmark, too, has a setback line of $100 \, m$[10]. The method proposed in Norfolk involves multiplying the rate at which a part of the coast is eroding by the planning horizon, and adding a safety margin to allow for landslips from cliff tops. This " variable definition setback line " would then be reviewed on a regular basis. As Dr Kay of the Environmental Risk Assessment Unit at East Anglia University points out, however, Norfolk's proposed policies raise important issues which need to be resolved: how to compensate land and property owners in areas which are no longer to be protected from the sea; how to determine the planning horizons of particular developments; how to explain and justify what is a radical new policy to the communities affected; how to determine flood risk areas in sufficient detail; and how to define " appropriate " defence standards for different developments. **We recommend that the Government build on its recent advice to authorities on sea level allowances for coastal defences and issue guidance on how to manage and resource abandon and retreat policies at the coast, including the role, design and implementation of setback lines, and how to compensate land and property owners in the areas affected.**

Controlled Retreat

89. We mentioned in paragraph 85 above that retreating from the existing line of coastal defences is one option in response to sea level rise. Various retreat strategies can be identified, ranging from the do-nothing option, through a minimum intervention approach, to the restoration

---

[1] " Flood threat to United Kingdom nuclear power plants ", *Hot News*, Climate Action Network—United Kingdom, Issue 5 Winter 1992.

[2] Appendix 7, Arun District Council (Evidence not printed).

[3] QQ 178, 180.

[4] East Sussex Coastal Group (Evidence not printed).

[5] Appendix 17.

[6] Appendix 18.

[7] *ibid.*

[8] Appendix 17.

[9] Dr Robert Kay, 1991, "Planning on a loss " in *Heritage Coast* Issue 6 December 1991.

[10] Per Roed Jakobson and Niels Tougaard, *Op cit.*

or recreation of habitats for nature conservation[1]. A true do-nothing approach is simply the abandonment of existing coastal defences, leaving an area entirely exposed to natural forces. "Controlled", "managed" or "strategic" retreat involves the implementation of engineering works and management techniques to create a desirable habitat.

90. Many witnesses argued the need for a policy of controlled retreat[2] on the grounds that it would replace wildlife habitats that have been lost to agriculture, that existing wildlife habitat may be lost as a result of squeezing the intertidal area between a rising low water mark and a hard coastal defence, that retreat may be more cost-effective than accepting an increased risk of flooding or investment in expensive capital works, that it would avoid the disruption of sediment patterns caused by coastal defences, and that land eroded by the sea in one area would be offset by accretion elsewhere. A study commissioned by the Countryside Commission, the NRA, the DOE and the then Nature Conservancy Council[3] concluded that

> "carefully planned, managed and monitored habitat restoration and creation projects could provide a means of significantly reducing the impact of both recorded and anticipated coastal habitat loss. Such artificially created habitats could, however, take upwards of 10 or 20 years to realise their maximum environmental value".

We believe that the concept of controlled retreat is an attractive one, but in need of further study and monitoring over the long term. We trust that the bodies which commissioned the Posford Duvivier report will seek to act on its conclusions. However, we appreciate that the report's qualification signifies that there are various obstacles to successfully implementing a policy of controlled retreat.

91. In the first instance, there is a lack of the necessary skills and understanding to recreate and manage natural wetland habitats on land encroached by the sea. We were told by English Nature that the main habitat that might be encroached upon for managed retreat is grazing marsh, and that whereas there may be the techniques to recreate the nature conservation value of the majority of these areas as saltmarsh to sustain their bird interest,

> "we do not currently have the techniques in a proven way—they are still very much in development and will need rather long time scales to prove that they are going to work—to bring back the floristic assemblages to areas that are wholly transferred"[4].

We appreciate that organisations such as the Institute of Terrestrial Ecology are monitoring coastal habitats, particularly saltmarshes and sand dunes in order to predict changes and management responses[5]. **We recommend that research and development be continued into the recreation of wildlife habitats from agricultural land at the coast and that monitoring of the changes in natural habitats be continued to provide a better basis of understanding for such work.**

92. Secondly, we appreciate that there are problems with evaluating whether land should be subject to a policy of abandonment, protection or retreat. As we were told by the Countryside Commission, this is an "incredibly difficult area"[6] and work is currently being commissioned to quantify the costs and benefits of retreat or protection options. We were told by the Flood Hazard Research Centre that "generally the protection of agricultural land is not economic"[7]. We were told by MAFF that "our schemes not only have to be cost-effective and also technically effective, but they also have to be cost beneficial"[8]. This involves evaluating the environmental or "intangible" costs and benefits of coastal defence options—the loss or gain in conservation, aesthetic or amenity terms for example, which are difficult to quantify in monetary terms. However, such quantifications will have to be formulated for effective decision-making on coastal retreat policies. **We recommend that in order for controlled retreat of coastal defences to become a realistic policy, progress be made in formulating cost/benefit analyses that include appropriate and acceptable quantifications of the environmental effects of coastal defence options.**

---

[1] Posford Duvivier Environment, 1991 *Environmental opportunities in low lying coastal areas under a scenario of climate change,* Countryside Commission.

[2] Evidence pp 93, 119, 138, 154, Appendices 15, 16, Countryside Council for Wales, Pembrokeshire Coast National Park, Soil Survey and Land Research Centre (Evidence not printed).

[3] Posford Duvivier Environment, *Op cit.*

[4] Q 403.

[5] Appendix 16.

[6] Q 435.

[7] Appendix 11.

[8] Q 227.

93. Finally, we appreciate that funding is a major impediment to relinquishing agricultural land to other uses. "Compensation" to farmers is a difficult issue, because as we were informed by MAFF officials, coastal authorities are under no obligation to provide coastal defences[1]. A different approach may be to pay farmers to accept another line of defence, for example, to manage their land that is reclaimed by the sea for conservation purposes. From our discussion with MAFF it was evident that the Government has not formed a definitive policy on this issue, and that whereas no payments as such are made at the moment, this is a development that may take place in the future[2]. We are aware that arrangements are already in place, such as set-aside schemes and the Country Stewardship Scheme[3] which encourage farmers to manage land for other ends than intensive agricultural production. **We recommend that the Government consider ways of resourcing the creation of new coastal habitats as an incentive for landowners to participate in a policy of controlled retreat.**

Financing Coastal Defence: Hard v Soft Engineering

94. Problems of finance are not confined to controlled retreat options; they apply to coastal defence policies as a whole. We received evidence that criticised the present grant aid procedures for being complex, for providing capital and not revenue grants, for obstructing programmed investment on a staged and sequential basis, and for the rate of grant being too low[4]. Mr Madden, Grade 3 for Environment Policy in MAFF, told us that the grants rates are being reviewed and increased where necessary[5], and that MAFF recognised that local authorities have problems with the funding and the carrying out of coastal defence work[6].

95. Our other main concern is the apparent confusion over capital and maintenance grants for coastal defences (especially in the case of storm damage[7]) and the allegation that the present funding system distorts spending in favour of " hard " over " soft " works[8]. We were told by MAFF that financial assistance is available where major maintenance involving a massive investment may be needed, and that soft defences involving beach rechargement can also qualify for grant[9]. When we questioned the ICE about the existing grant aid system, they confirmed that until the last 10 years or so, grant aid was not available for soft defences. Traditionally, " things have been allowed to drift until you have actually got a real problem which you called in to try to address and then, almost implicitly, you are faced with a hard solution "[10]. In the ICE's opinion, " a soft solution will be just as effective in the long term as a multi-million pound hard solution "[11].

96. Many witnesses have argued that soft coastal defences are preferable to large-scale, capital-intensive hard structures because they aim to work with rather than against the natural coastal processes[12]. From our own inspection of coastal defence schemes in Sefton[13], **we agree that a general preference for soft defences is to be welcomed, but this should be tempered by a need to ensure both fitness for purpose, and more fundamentally, that the design of any defence system is based on a sound knowledge of the natural processes.** We realise that the legacy of the coastal defence funding system in the United Kingdom is not conducive to soft coastal engineering. **We recommend that the Government continue to review its funding arrangements for coastal defence works with a view to promoting rather than discouraging the use of soft engineered schemes, and supporting the maintenance and repair as well as the capital costs of all coastal defences.**

---

[1] Q 229.

[2] Q 231.

[3] The Countryside Commission, 1991, *The Coast,* Landscape Management Leaflet.

[4] Evidence p 251, Appendices 2, 3, 17, Christchurch Borough Council, Swansea Bay Study Group (Evidence not printed).

[5] Q 257. Grant rates are proposed to rise to 85 per cent for sea defence and 75 per cent for coast protection. Present levels are 60 per cent each.

[6] Q 258.

[7] Q 835.

[8] Appendix 2. Hard defences include structures such as sea walls, revetments, groynes. Soft defences include beach replenishment, sand dune restoration, offshore breakwaters.

[9] Q 165.

[10] Q 746.

[11] *ibid.*

[12] Evidence pp 93, 153,173, 251, Appendices 3, 7, 12, Arun DC, Countryside Council for Wales, The Marine Technology Directorate Limited, Pembrokeshire Coast National Park Authority (Evidence not printed).

[13] At Formby point, Christmas trees and fencing are used to trap sand and therefore prevent dune erosion (the preferred option to constructing a concrete wall), but this practice is a continuing drain on the Council's expenditure, Evidence p 260.

97. Finally, we wish to comment on the source of material for beach replenishment schemes. When we questioned the British Ports Federation, we found out that ports dredge and deposit at sea almost 41 million tonnes of material in the course of programmes for maintaining the safety of navigation channels in ports and harbours[1]. We were told by Sir David Scott of Civil and Marine Limited[2] that the total amount of material removed from harbours in England and Wales as a result of maintenance dredging approximates 80 million tonnes, compared to the total of 26 million tonnes from capital dredging of sand and gravel. According to Dr Brampton from HR Wallingford, the environmental effects of maintenance dredging are greater than those of capital dredging[3]. We were therefore concerned to learn that harbour maintenance dredging requires no prior study into coast erosion or environmental effects[4]. Where dredged material is uncontaminated, we perceive the environmental benefits of recycling it, for example, by using it for schemes such as beach replenishment[5] since we also found out that these schemes presently rely on the marine aggregate industry[6]. We were told by the British Ports Federation that other beneficial uses of dredgings include land and landfill reclamations, brick making and as aggregates for construction, but that these form " a relatively small proportion of the material that is dredged "[7]. Where dredged material is contaminated we were told it was pumped inshore into lagoons or dumped at sea[8]. It seemed clear, however, that little is done to assess the impact of this material on the environment to which it is taken[9]. Also, there is no point of reference to which people engaged in dredging can turn for advice, either as to the impact of this material on the environment, or as to the possibility of using it for beneficial purposes. MAFF, in issuing its licences for dumping, seems to be primarily concerned with the effect of dumping on fish and crustaceans, and does not appear to undertake any wider environmental impact assessment. **We recommend that there should be better co-ordination between those authorities responsible for dredging, disposing of and utilising marine aggregates in order to avoid the unnecessary dumping of dredged material, and to encourage its use elsewhere as appropriate. In addition, we recommend that environmental impact assessments be made of the possible effects of dumping, and that the DOE issue guidance notes as to the possible harmful effects of dredged material and the alternative beneficial uses to which it can be put.**

---

[1] This total is for England and Wales and based on 138 licences (1989 figures).
[2] Appendix 9.
[3] Appendix 29.
[4] *ibid.*
[5] *ibid.*
[6] Q 750.
[7] Q 663.
[8] Q 665.
[9] QQ 669–671.

NATURE CONSERVATION IN THE COASTAL ZONE

Nature Conservation Designations

98. The coast is not only a distinctive feature of the United Kingdom's landscape, but coastal habitats are home for many internationally important species of plants and animals[1]. Landscape and wildlife conservation are the responsibilities of the DOE, and of the territorial Departments. Policy is implemented in England largely through the Countryside Commission (for landscape) and English Nature (for wildlife) and their equivalent bodies in Scotland and Wales[2]. The evidence we received from the DOE explains in more detail the history of landscape and wildlife conservation in the United Kingdom, and the various protections and designations that occur in the coastal zone[3].

99. The most significant forms of statutory landscape protection to be found in English coastal areas include National Parks and Areas of Outstanding Natural Beauty (AONBs); and the relevant wildlife designations include Sites of Special Scientific Interest (SSSIs), National Nature Reserves, Local Nature Reserves, Marine Nature Reserves, Special Protection Areas and Ramsar sites. Heritage Coasts provide a further layer of non-statutory protection for many stretches of the coast.

100. There were two things that struck us about the existing arrangements for nature conservation in the coastal zone: first, there are numerous forms of designation for the landward side of the coastal zone; second, despite this array of protected areas, conservationists are not satisfied with the degree of protection afforded to them. The main cause for concern is that there is only one type of statutory designation that provides for the conservation of *marine* areas, the Marine Nature Reserve (MNR)[4]. None of the other designations affords protection below the low water mark[5]. MNR designation, however, has been criticised as slow (only two sites have been designated in 10 years)[6], " very unsatisfactory "[7], not set into any wider management context for the surrounding sea areas, and not perceived to have any benefits beyond nature conservation[8]. Such criticisms concern us because we looked at the problem of designating marine conservation seven years ago[9]. At that time we recommended that " as a matter of urgency ", the DOE and MAFF take action to break the deadlock in designating MNRs by giving the then NCC or the Secretary of State adequate powers to set up Marine Nature Reserves.[10]

101. We are aware that the Government has expressed an intention to review existing legislation of relevance to marine conservation[11] and has recently published a consultation paper on Marine Consultation Areas for England and Wales[12]. We were told by the Marine Conservation Society, however, that the experience of Marine Consultation Areas in Scotland has been " rather unsatisfactory " and that the MCA approach is " neither one thing or another ". That is, it is neither voluntary in that it includes public involvement in working out effective management agreements, nor is it statutory with " sufficient teeth "[13]. Instead, we were requested to support a more unified approach known as " Marine Protected Areas " which aims to integrate nature conservation objectives within the wider planning and management of the marine environment, and which looks after the interests of a number of groups, including fishing, recreational and archaeological interests[14]. **We are disappointed that there has been no progress with protecting marine conservation areas since our recommendation on this issue seven years ago. We recommend that when the Government reviews marine conservation legislation it explore approaches other than those of Marine Nature Reserves and Marine Consultation Areas which have so far proved to be unsatisfactory and unworkable. The wider concept of Marine Protected Areas should be one of the options considered.**

---

[1] Evidence p 9.

[2] Countryside Council for Wales, Countryside Commission for Scotland and the Nature Conservancy Council for Scotland (which will be combined to form Scottish Natural Heritage from 1 April 1992). In Northern Ireland, the DOE(NI) has responsibility for nature and countryside conservation.

[3] Evidence pp 9–11.

[4] Evidence p 84.

[5] Evidence pp 136, 253, Appendix 15.

[6] QQ 71, 298.

[7] Royal Institution of Chartered Surveyors (Evidence not printed).

[8] Evidence p 84.

[9] Operation and Effectiveness of Part II of the Wildlife and Countryside Act, HC 6–I 1984–85.

[10] *ibid*, paragraph 72.

[11] *This Common Inheritance, Op cit.*

[12] *Marine Consultation Areas: a Consultation Paper* by the Department of the Environment and the Welsh Office, February 1992.

[13] Q 298.

[14] *ibid.*

102. The other major problem with conservation in the coastal zone, as we mentioned in paragraph 100, is that the current system does not allow statutory designations to cross the land/sea divide[1]. The WWF illustrated the inadequacies of such an arrangement when they told us that sea birds on St Kilda are protected when on land, but "the area that they are feeding in has no protection whatsoever"[2]. The problem extends even to international designations such as Ramsar and SPA sites because their coverage has been limited to the areas of existing SSSIs by Government[3]. Several witnesses expressed concern that because the protection afforded by SSSIs is questionable below the low water mark, the United Kingdom may not be fulfilling its international conservation obligations[4]. When we asked English Nature how the present arrangements could be amended, its Chief Executive, Dr Derek Langslow suggested extending "an SSSI-type mechanism" because he did not believe that "simply translating what is presently in the 1981 Act[5] directly into a new statute below the low water mark would be the best way of handling the detail of it"[6]. Significantly, he thought the Marine Nature Reserve framework would not be appropriate in most situations to fill the "legislative gap"[7]. **We are concerned that the conservation of areas below the low water mark is hampered by the inability of landward designations to straddle the land/sea divide. This problem is ultimately linked to the wider issue of planning regimes in the coastal zone, which we dealt with in previous recommendations[8]. We recommend that in its review of marine conservation legislation, the Government address the issue of how to link conservation of land and sea areas, how to protect sites of marine conservation importance, and consider as an option extending SSSI-type mechanisms below the low water mark.**

Protective Ownership of Coastal Land

103. Landscape and wildlife designations are not the only means of safeguarding the character of the coastal zone. We were told that "the ultimate form of safeguard is protective ownership in some way"[9]. The ownership and conservation management of coastal land is a practice employed by some local authorities[10], and on a national scale by organisations such as the National Trust and the RSPB. The same effects as protective ownership can also be achieved by lease, licence or management agreements. In 1965, the National Trust launched its Enterprise Neptune Appeal with the aim of securing 900 miles of unspoilt coastline and adjoining land. Today, the Trust owns 473 miles of coastline (91,000 acres of coastal land) and protects a further 52 miles (23,500 acres) by covenant[11]. The National Trust's memorandum of evidence describes the policies and management systems that operate for these areas.

104. The National Trust's practice of purchasing land in order to protect it in perpetuity has been used as a model by other countries. For example, it is mirrored across the channel by the Conservatoire de L'Espace Littoral[12] (the Conservatoire), the main difference between the two systems being that the French body administers the purchase of sites and their conveyance to the appropriate local authority which then becomes the managing agent. In the United Kingdom, the National Trust remains both owner and manager. **We recommend that the Government actively facilitate the acquisition of coastal land by appropriate organisations, supported by sensitive management agreements as options for protecting the natural fabric of the coastal zone. Such a policy might be developed by a national coastal zone unit.**

The "Urban" Coast

105. In the majority of cases, landscape and nature conservation designations focus on the "wilder" parts of the coast. Witnesses have pointed out that the value of the wider coastline and coastal areas close to urban centres should also be recognised[13]. To a large extent, the protection of

---

[1] Evidence p 84.

[2] Q 373.

[3] *ibid;* DOE Circular 27/87 Nature Conservation.

[4] Evidence pp 84, 120, 132, 136, 156, Appendix 4.

[5] The Wildlife and Countryside Act 1981.

[6] Q 400.

[7] *ibid.*

[8] *See* Paragraphs 49, 51 and 52 above.

[9] Q 452.

[10] Such as Hampshire CC, Appendix 13.

[11] Evidence p 88.

[12] The French State Coastal Conservancy.

[13] Evidence p 254, Countryside Commission, 1991, *Heritage Coasts: policies and priorities 1991,* CCP 305.

the undeveloped coast will rely on the effectiveness of development control policies. Alternatively, the protection of the unspoiled coast is helped by the proper use of the developed coast[1].

106. When asked, various witnesses disagreed with the DOE's statement that the undeveloped coast is " well protected by the planning system "[2]. Rather, the National Trust believed that even AONBs and Heritage Coasts " do not prevent development occurring within those areas "[3]. Several witnesses recommended a presumption against development which may affect the unspoilt coastline[4]; we heard from Dr Shaw, Director of the Centre for Marine and Coastal Studies at Liverpool University that only " necessary " development should be permitted on the coast[5]; others recommended the development or renewal of areas already developed (such as the conversion of redundant land or docks for moorings) in order to ease the pressure on other areas[6]. When we visited the Sefton Coast, for example, we were told by Mr Tim Cox, Borough Planning Officer, that the Council favoured what he termed a " re-cycling " or renewal of seaside resorts (such as we saw at Southport beach) rather than a spread of new seaside developments onto undeveloped coastlines[7]. **We believe that the conservation of the coastal zone should be a general aim, and not confined to the finest stretches of the coastline nor to the most important sites of wildlife importance. We recommend that the Government give a strong lead on the protection of the coastal resource as a whole.**

Pollution

107. Marine pollution of various sorts has been the subject of previous Reports by this Committee[8]. It has also been the concern of conservation bodies like the then Nature Conservancy Council which produced an atlas of coastal conservation sites sensitive to oil pollution[9] in order to aid the Marine Pollution Control Unit[10] and local authorities with oil spill clean-up. Since pollution of the coastal zone stems from both landward and seaward activities, pollution control arrangements are complex and spread over several Government Departments. Full details are given in the Department's memorandum[11].

108. We recently considered existing responsibilities from marine pollution in our Report on the proposed Environment Agency[12]. We concluded that we wished to see a broader approach to controlling inshore pollution and the dumping of waste at sea, and that such a " grey area " as it currently stands should be reviewed by the Government for possible inclusion within the Environment Agency. We are not alone in wishing to see some review of responsibility for pollution in the coastal zone. The RTPI suggested that pollution control should be vested in one authority, the proposed Environment Agency[13]; Wildlife Link raised searching questions as to who takes the lead responsibility for oil or chemical spills in estuaries under various different scenarios[14]. When we asked DOE officials about pollution control arrangements, we were told that

> "as to the general principles, I believe these are clear enough … In practice of course incidents do not necessarily divide neatly in that particular way … the lead responsibility depends on a number of factors, principally the source, scale and location of the spillage "[15].

109. The Government's current approach is to rely on contingency plans which co-ordinate the roles of the different bodies in specific circumstances, and at our request, the DOE provided us with a supplementary note on national and local contingency planning[16]. **We believe that with the establishment of the proposed Environment Agency, the whole area of marine pollution control is in**

---

[1] Q 827.

[2] Evidence p 4.

[3] Q 292.

[4] Evidence pp 40, 90, 169, Countryside Council for Wales (Evidence not printed).

[5] Appendix 7.

[6] Evidence p 38, Appendix 7, The British Marine Industries Federation (Evidence not printed).

[7] Q 827.

[8] HC 183 1986–87, HC 22 1988–89, HC 12 1989–90.

[9] *Atlas of nature conservation sites in Great Britain sensitive to coastal oil pollution*, NCC.

[10] The MCPU is part of the Department of Transport.

[11] Evidence pp 12–14.

[12] HC 55 1991–92.

[13] Evidence p 41.

[14] Evidence p 130.

[15] Q 54.

[16] Appendix 22 Annex D.

need of review. We therefore repeat the recommendation of our previous Report on the Environment Agency and urge the Government to consider whether responsibility for marine pollution control, which is at present dispersed across several Departments, would be better invested in one lead body, and whether the Environment Agency could fulfil that central role.

110. Finally, we wish to comment on a particular case of marine pollution which concerned us in one of our previous Reports[1]. During our inquiry on Toxic Waste, we visited Seaham Harbour in County Durham and saw the appalling effects of colliery spoil and slurry disposal on the beach. During the course of our current inquiry we heard that the Marine Conservation Society has just completed a survey of the coast in that area and could confirm that the sea bed has been grossly polluted a number of miles offshore—"some of the worst, most obvious direct smothering contamination effects you will see anywhere in the country on an area of sea bed"[2]. In a memorandum submitted by British Coal[3], we were informed that MAFF will not be renewing British Coal's licence to dispose of minewaste on the North Sea coast beyond 1995 unless the planning system shows that no land-based method of disposal exists. **We recommend that greater effort be made to find alternative means of disposing of colliery spoil and slurry than dumping such waste in the coastal zone, and that the deadline of 1995 be made absolute and not conditional.**

Fishing

111. We decided at the beginning of this inquiry that we would not be focusing on fish farming or the fishing industry, partly because this is an area in which the DOE has no policy responsibility (and therefore outside our remit as the Departmental Select Committee), partly because our colleagues on the Agriculture Select Committee have recently inquired into Fish Farming in the United Kingdom[4], and partly because fish farming is predominantly based in Scotland, which is again outwith the scope of the present inquiry. We do have a continuing interest, however, in the environmental effects of fishing methods. When we considered Environmental Issues in Northern Ireland[5], for example, we were very disturbed to find that large areas of Strangford Lough has been turned into a moonscape by the "hoovering-up" of scallops along the sea bed by trawlers. We therefore recommended that the Government protect the Lough from irrevocable damage by large-scale fishing operations. The Government responded by saying it would consider legislation to effect restrictions on methods of fishing in the Lough and to limit fishing to certain areas and specific seasons[6]. We are aware that the Sea Fisheries (Wildlife Conservation) Act 1992 requires appropriate Ministers and local fisheries committees or any authority exercising the powers of such committees to have regard to the conservation of marine flora and fauna and to endeavour to achieve a reasonable balance between conservation and "any other considerations to which he is or they are required to have regard" in the discharge of their functions under the Sea Fisheries Acts[7].

112. On a wider scale, we were told by witnesses from English Nature that trawling in the Irish and North Seas has essentially changed the nature of the benthic communities (communities on the sea bed) to the effect that they are not necessarily less valuable, but "they are certainly losing diversity"[8]. That organisation was in favour of less damaging methods of scallop collection in particular, and in general, a policy of zoning areas depending on their sensitivity to fishing operations. For example, highly sensitive areas could be set aside either for low intensity fishing or even fishing exclusion zones. In areas of "middle importance", they believed that less damaging fishing methods should be found[9]. The NRA also "supports the need for the zoning of uses to facilitate water quality management"[10].

113. We perceive the balance that needs to be struck between protecting on the one hand the richness and diversity of the marine environment and on the other, the livelihoods of fishermen and related industries. We were interested in Dr Shaw's presentation to us that there seems to be a marked contrast between the levels of Government support given to fishermen who find it difficult

---

[1] HC 22 1988–89.

[2] Q 319.

[3] British Coal (Evidence not printed).

[4] HC 141 1989–90.

[5] HC 39 1990–91.

[6] Cm 1484.

[7] Bill 34 1991–92, presented by Mr Phillip Oppenheim MP.

[8] Q 404.

[9] QQ 404–5.

[10] Evidence p 62.

to make a living and that given to farmers[1]. The Association of Sea Fisheries Committees has indicated to us that Sea Fisheries Committees[2] have a role to play in helping to achieve a balance between fishing and the environment and to foster good working relationships between conservation and fishing interests[3]. **We recommend that the Government seek to achieve a balance between the exploitation of fish and shellfish in the coastal zone and marine habitat and wildlife conservation. Zoning of coastal fishing waters according to sensitivity with the assistance of the Sea Fisheries Committees, the Shellfish Association of Great Britain, MAFF, the NRA and conservation bodies would be one option.**

114. As regards the issue of fish farming in the coastal zone, we were concerned to hear that in certain circumstances fish farms cause pollution[4]. The Agriculture Select Committee was concerned enough about this problem and the fact that monitoring methodology " is not fully developed " to recommend in its Report[5] that the Scottish Office and the River Purification Boards should undertake a review of procedures to ensure that water quality is properly protected. We were prompted to ask whether fish farms should not become subject to planning regulations, even though they are located below the low water mark, and therefore beyond the jurisdiction of the planning authorities[6]? We were already aware that the RTPI believes that fish farming should be brought under planning control[7]. The Crown Estate responded to our question by explaining to us the existing arrangement for fish farm licences in Scotland[8], whereby the Department of Agriculture consults widely on applications, with appeals being decided by an appellate committee. **We appreciate that the regulatory procedure for fish farms has been reviewed and improved in recent years, but we believe that there is still a case for bringing fish farming within the direct control of elected planning authorities. We recommend that the Government consider the desirability of such a policy as part of a wider review of extending planning controls below the low water mark. In addition, we recommend that the environmental effects of fisheries be monitored, particularly in inshore areas.**

[1] Appendix 7.

[2] Sea Fisheries Committees are statutory bodies set up circa 1890 to manage and develop the coastal sea fisheries. They operate under the Sea Fisheries Regulation Act 1966, and are made up of representatives from the maritime local authorities, MAFF, NRA, commercial fishermen, Appendix 5.

[3] Appendix 5.

[4] Q 501.

[5] *Op cit*, paragraph 74.

[6] Q 502.

[7] Evidence p 38.

[8] Q 504.

COASTAL ZONE MANAGEMENT

Definition of Coastal Zone Management

115. This final section deals with the subject of "Coastal Zone Management", an approach which attempts to provide solutions to the problems involved with coastal zone protection and planning, and which therefore provides a fitting conclusion to our Report. If Coastal Zone Management represents the integrated planning and management of the coastal zone, then it is an approach which we have urged (although not specifically named as such) throughout our Report, and it is one that is gaining support in a number of maritime nations. Most significantly, it is an approach favoured by the European Commission which, as we have noted[1], is preparing a Communication that is expected to advocate compulsory strategies for the coastal zone.

116. Definitions of Coastal Zone Management (CZM) differ between countries, but a common factor is that basic environmental principles underlie the whole process. A detailed discussion of the mechanics and benefits of CZM is given in Gubbay, 1990[2]. As we were told by the Marine Conservation Society, Coastal Zone Management was defined by the Coastal Area Management and Planning Network[3] in 1989 as

> "a dynamic process in which a co-ordinated strategy is developed and implemented for the allocation of environmental, socio-cultural and institutional resources to achieve the conservation and sustainable multiple use of the coastal zone "[4].

117. The importance of Coastal Zone Management is that it aims to integrate *all* uses and activities in the coastal zone, not just coastal defence or conservation alone. Its main objectives are to promote sustainable use of the coast; balance demands for coastal zone resources; resolve conflicts of use; promote environmentally sensitive use of the coastal zone; and promote strategic planning of the coast[5]. Coastal Zone Management recognises the coastal zone as a unit for planning purposes, and that planning and management of coastal land and waters cannot be dealt with separately. In order to function effectively, CZM requires a national perspective, a long-term view, an integrated approach to planning and management, co-ordination and co-operation between planners, managers and users, and a specific agency to deal with coastal zone matters[6]. We have been urged to support Coastal Zone Management by many of our witnesses[7]. **We recognise the benefits of the approach known as Coastal Zone Management, and we recommend that such an approach be adopted as the framework for all coastal zone planning and management practices in the United Kingdom.**

Coastal Zone Management Plans

118. Coastal Zone Management relies for implementation on a system of integrated Coastal Zone Management Plans at different levels of resolution. We have already discussed the need for a national coastal strategy which would provide an overall framework for the development of coastal zone policy[8]. This national CZM Plan would deal with issues that require a national overview, such as co-ordinating response strategies to sea level rise, port development and rehabilitation, tidal power development, and measures for introducing sustainable coastal zone policies and programmes.

119. The second tier for implementing CZM would consist of regional Coastal Zone Management Plans. These documents would provide the strategic framework for the regional coastal "cells" that we identified in paragraph 42, and would extend inland and out to sea as far as the issues demanded—the pragmatic approach that we recommended in paragraph 18. It is inevitable that such regional Plans would straddle district, county and even national boundaries. We were told by the Institution of Civil Engineers that the Liverpool Bay Group already covers

---

[1] *See* Paragraph 24 above.

[2] *Op cit.*

[3] The Coastal Area Management and Planning Network (CAMPNET), 1989, *The Status of Integrated Coastal Zone Management*, Rosential School of Marine Science, University of Miami, Florida.

[4] Evidence p 86.

[5] *ibid.*

[6] *ibid.*

[7] Evidence pp 83, 125, 135, 254, Appendices 4, 5, 8, 12, 14, Heritage Coast Forum, London Boroughs Association, NCC for Scotland (Evidence not printed).

[8] *See* Paragraph 39 above.

part of England and Wales, and that the system " works perfectly well "[1]. On a topic basis, regional Coastal Zone Management Plans should cover all coastal issues relevant to the area, examples of which we listed in paragraph 15.

120. Finally, within the wider regional strategy, we see the need for local Coastal Zone Management Plans—what the RSPB has called " whole estuary " or " coastal subject plans "[2]—which would set objectives and management arrangements for smaller geographical units such as beaches, estuaries or Heritage Coasts, depending on coastal topographic boundaries[3]. We understand that English Nature will be instituting a programme of management plan preparation for individual estuaries in 1992–93, aiming to cover 80 per cent of the estuarial area of England by 2000[4].

121. While there may not be examples of Coastal Zone Management Plans in the United Kingdom (the nearest we have are Hampshire County Council's coastal strategy[5], Sefton Metropolitan Borough Council's Coast Management Scheme[6]—now incorporated in the Borough's draft Unitary Development Plan, the " Framework Plans " prepared by the Highland Regional Council[7] for some of the sea lochs, and the Northumberland Coast Management Plan (at the consultation stage)), we see such existing initiatives as the " building blocks "[8] of a CZM Plan framework. We know that a more developed system of CZM Plans exists in France and in Denmark. In France, the State operates the Schemas de Mise en Valeur de la Mer (SMVMs) which are essentially statutory local Coastal Zone Management Plans and which enable local authorities to develop plans for estuarial and coastal areas where there is a need to resolve conflicts of use. In Denmark, the National Agency for Physical Planning has produced a Circular on the planning and administration of coastal areas that provides a framework for regional, municipal and local planning[9].

122. We received wide-ranging support for a " cascade " of Coastal Zone Management Plans[10]. Opinions differed, however, on how CZM Plans should relate to the existing statutory plan system. The ICE and the Anglian Coastal Authorities Group argued in good engineering tradition that the Plans should be built " from the foundations upwards "[11], so that local CZM Plans feed into the Structure Plan system. Such a " bottom up " approach is akin to the process adopted by Sefton MBC, which has had to act in the absence of any regional strategy and has incorporated the policies of its Coast Management Scheme into its draft Unitary Development Plan (UDP). The Countryside Commission favoured the idea of non-statutory regional CZM Plans on the lines of the Rural (Countryside) Strategies now being prepared by a number of County Councils to achieve similar co-ordination of policies and action programmes in the countryside as a whole[12]. The Commission also drew attention to the non-statutory area-based Heritage Coast management plans which could become component parts of the wider CZM Plans[13]. Both the Commission and the RSPB argued for the retention of Subject Plans within the statutory Development Plans system as a vehicle for providing statutory guidance for the coastal zone[14]. The RTPI made a distinction between planning and management of the coast—between statutory subject plans for coasts and non-statutory local management plans[15]. The RTPI's favoured approach would be for interested bodies (including adjacent local authorities) to produce local coastal management plans which would then be incorporated into district-wide Local Plans[16].

---

[1] Q 694.

[2] Evidence p 112.

[3] Q 354.

[4] Evidence p 160.

[5] *A Strategy for Hampshire's Coast,* 1991, Hampshire CC, Winchester.

[6] Evidence p 253.

[7] Evidence p 85.

[8] Q 785.

[9] *Draft Circular on planning and administration of coastal areas (for county councils and municipal councils),* 1991, National Agency for Physical Planning Denmark, P 111–0010 IV/rbj.

[10] Evidence pp 40, 85, 113, 139, 158, Appendices 1, 3, 7, 8, 12, 15, 20, Countryside Council for Wales, Irish Sea Study Group, Nature Conservancy Council for Scotland, Pembrokeshire Coast National Park Authority (Evidence not printed).

[11] QQ 686, 705.

[12] Appendix 20.

[13] *ibid.*

[14] Evidence p 112, Appendix 20.

[15] Q 125.

[16] *ibid.*

123. The statutory context of Coastal Zone Management Plans is a complex issue. Probably the most helpful ideas came from officers from Sefton MBC who argued the need for a combination of both local experience and strategic direction[1]. We agree with Sefton MBC that a balance needs to be struck between a "cascading down" from the strategic level of national and regional Coastal Zone Management Plans to coastal zone management at the local level, and a "bottom up" approach whereby locally-driven policies and experiences gain importance through incorporation within the statutory Development Plan system. This necessarily demands a flexible and pragmatic approach. A possible model for this process is the system for producing strategic and regional guidance for the land use planning system[2].

124. A further consideration on the subject of Coastal Zone Management Plans is how potentially conflicting policies, say between different authorities on opposite sides of an estuary, can be resolved. The Marine Conservation Society was confident that the Coastal Zone Management approach provided a "framework for constructive debate"[3], in the sense that the Groups preparing the plans would be a means for bringing the parties together. As we were told by officers from Sefton MBC, there is at the moment "no adequate framework for them to come together and there is no adequate way of actually dealing with the problems"[4]. However, if an *impasse* were reached, the Marine Conservation Society saw the matter being referred in the first instance to the national coastal zone unit, but if the situation was still unresolved, a final decision resting with the Secretary of State[5].

125. **We recommend that there should be a hierarchy of Coastal Zone Management Plans from the national to regional and local levels. We believe these Plans should be non-statutory documents, but that their policies should be incorporated in the relevant Development Plans, and that the grant-aid policies of the organisations concerned with the coast are linked to this strategic framework. We recommend that the Government issue guidance on how CZM Plans are to be prepared, by whom, and what they should cover.**

Coastal Zone Management Groups

126. If Coastal Management Plans are intended to cover all uses and activities in the coastal zone, we believe it is essential that all interested parties are involved in preparing those Plans. We are aware that there are currently very few multi-agency groups or fora on a regional or local basis that are interested in all the issues involved in Coastal Zone Management. There are more examples of groups with a more limited range of responsibilities (for example, the Marine Pollution Information Forum or the engineering-based Regional Coastal Groups). In paragraphs 40 to 42 we discussed the existing voluntary Regional Coastal Groups, and we concluded that with some changes in membership and a reorganisation on a coastal cell basis, they could form a useful foundation on which to build Coastal Zone Management Groups. For example, the geographical extent of each group should be based on the configuration of the coast and the interaction of the natural coastal processes, and not based on administrative boundaries.

127. We were therefore interested to hear on our visit to Sefton[6] about the Irish Sea Forum and the Mersey Estuary Project Group. The Irish Sea Study[7] spurred the local authorities around the Irish Sea to establish a Forum to continue the work initiated by the Study. The Forum secretariat is to be funded by the local authority grouping and will liaise with the Irish Sea Science Co-ordinator to be appointed by the DOE. The Estuary Group of the Mersey Basin Campaign comprises a wide range of public and private sector agencies and has provided the impetus for an estuary Management Plan that will cover six main topic areas—navigation, development and transport, pollution and hazards, recreation, wildlife and nature conservation and fisheries, land drainage and coast protection[8].

---

[1] Q 792.

[2] Such as PPG 12 February 1992, *Development Plans and Regional Planning Guidance*, paragraphs 2.2–2.3

[3] Q 273.

[4] Q 791.

[5] QQ 274–278.

[6] Evidence p 260.

[7] Irish Sea Study Group, 1990, *The Irish Sea: an environmental review* Volumes 1 to 4, Liverpool University Press.

[8] Presentation to the Committee by Dr David Massey, Department of Civic Design, University of Liverpool. The University provides the technical secretariat to the Mersey Estuary Project Group for the Management Plan Initiative, Evidence p 260.

128. There would need to be some lead authority or body for each regional or local Coastal Zone Management Plan—at the very least to provide a secretariat. In most cases one of the planning authorities[1] would probably be the most suitable, as it can adopt an overall view of coastal issues, but in some cases the lead could come from the NRA[2] or even, for local CZM Plans, bodies like the National Trust, depending on where the expertise and enthusiasm lie.

129. The constitution of the regional Groups would also vary according to local circumstances. For instance, elected Council members are represented on SCOPAC, but not on the Liverpool Bay Group, and yet both approaches appear to work satisfactorily[3]. The important issue is that the decisions of the regional CZM Groups are communicated back to the local authorities and other involved parties via the officers or members[4] in a clear and accountable way.

130. Finally, we appreciate that the effectiveness of the regional CZM Groups and, in a sense, of Coastal Zone Management as a whole, in tackling coastal problems, particularly those that cross administrative boundaries, will rely on people's collective goodwill. The human relationships issue is an important one. As we were told by officers from Sefton MBC, they had been " fortunate " in that the steering group for their Coast Management Scheme had developed good working relationships, aided by a relatively simple pattern of land ownership[5]. They thought it would be " gross optimism " to assume that such a voluntary system would work consistently well across the whole of the British Coast[6]. However, access to the same scientific information and " something in common "—be it aims, coastal visitors or coastal landscapes—were stressed as being conducive to successful partnerships[7].

131. **We recommend that the Government consider how best to establish, resource and empower regional Coastal Zone Management Groups based on natural coastal "cells" as the linchpin of integrated protection and planning of the coastal zone.**

---

[1] Q 796.

[2] Q 356.

[3] QQ 698–701.

[4] Q 700.

[5] Q 796.

[6] ibid.

[7] ibid.

PROCEEDINGS OF THE COMMITTEE
RELATING TO THE REPORT

THURSDAY 12 MARCH 1992

Members present:

Sir Hugh Rossi, in the Chair.

Mr John Cummings	Mr Robert B Jones
Mr Barry Field	Mr Tom Pendry
Mr Ralph Howell	Mr Anthony Steen

The Committee deliberated.

Draft Report (Coastal Zone Protection and Planning), proposed by the Chairman, brought up and read.

Ordered, That the draft Report be read a second time, paragraph by paragraph.

Paragraphs 1 to 131 read and agreed to.

Resolved, That the Report be the Second Report of the Committee to the House.

Ordered, That the Chairman do make the Report to the House.

Ordered, That the provisions of Standing Order No 116 (Select Committees (reports)) be applied to the Report.

Several papers were ordered to be appended to the Minutes of Evidence.

Ordered, That the Appendices to the Minutes of Evidence taken before the Committee be reported to the House.—*(The Chairman.)*

Several Memoranda were ordered to be reported to the House.

———————

Printed in the UK by HMSO
Dd 0202904 C7 4/92 3219695 19542

ISBN 0-10-290492-8

9 780102 904925